Frank Ried Diffenderffer

The German exodus to England in 1709

(Massen-Auswanderung der Pfälzer)

Frank Ried Diffenderffer

The German exodus to England in 1709
(Massen-Auswanderung der Pfälzer)

ISBN/EAN: 9783742845306

Manufactured in Europe, USA, Canada, Australia, Japa

Cover: Foto ©ninafisch / pixelio.de

Manufactured and distributed by brebook publishing software (www.brebook.com)

Frank Ried Diffenderffer

The German exodus to England in 1709

THE
GERMAN EXODUS TO ENGLAND
IN 1709.

(Massen-auswanderung der Pfälzer).

PREPARED AT THE REQUEST OF

The Pennsylvania-German Society.

BY FRANK RIED DIFFENDERFFER.

MEMBER OF THE PENNSYLVANIA-GERMAN SOCIETY; HISTORICAL SOCIETY OF PENNSYLVANIA; SECRETARY LANCASTER COUNTY HISTORICAL SOCIETY, ETC., ETC.

LANCASTER, PA.
1897.

INTRODUCTORY.

INSIGNIA OF THE PENNSYL-
VANIA-GERMAN SOCIETY.

THE colonization of this continent by the Spaniards, English, Dutch, Swedes, French and Germans, presents many curious historical features and incidents. From the settlement of the Spaniards in Central and South America, to that of the French in the Canadas, many curious episodes thrust themselves upon the consideration of the chronicler, matching in interest and importance anything told in Greek or Roman story.

Our Society, while taking an interest in all these early colonists, has to do only with those peoples from whom our membership claims descent, except in so far as they may incidentally have come into contact with the people of other races and their own lives and careers been influenced by the men of other lands, and whose interests and destinies were more or less closely interwoven with their own.

But even as we stand upon the very threshold of this great question of Germanic immigration and settlement in the New World, we are confronted with the magnitude no less than the importance and grandeur of the subject. Its period of active and continuous duration covers more than a century, and even now, more than two centuries since the first German settlement was made in one of the suburbs of Philadelphia, this Teutonic wave still continues to reach the shores of our Commonwealth. De Quincy in one of his brilliant essays describes the flight of a Tartar tribe, in which 600,000 men, women and children, pursued their course from the banks of the Volga, for more than 2000 miles through the treeless plains and sandy wastes that mark the highlands of Central Asia, from midwinter until the succeeding fall. It was an event wonderful in its conception and as remarkable for its successful execution. But it was after all, only the return of a people to the home which their forefathers had left generations before. It was going back to the old rooftrees where plenty as well as a welcome awaited them. Not so with the early Germans who came to America. Desolation and hunger indeed, lay behind them. With poverty and misery for companions, they braved the perils of the ocean for months at a time ; they were crowded into ships that became pest houses, in which the fatal

Introductory.

ship fever more than decimated their ranks, the survivors well aware that years of servitude under task masters would be their lot.

But the task to which I address myself is not to rehearse the story of the German immigration and settlement in this and some of the other states. That is a grand theme, worthy of anyone's ambition. In a general way it has been told and retold, but the subject is of fadeless interest and much still remains to be discovered and recorded. Out of the many interesting phases of this wonderful story, I have chosen one episode, one of which the writers of our history have made but small account, but which, while surrounded by obscurity, is nevertheless of surpassing interest to us, the descendants of those early colonists.

IMMIGRATION BEGINS.

EARLY GERMAN COLONISTS TO AMERICA—WHEN AND WHERE LOCATED—FOLLOWED BY THE STILL GREATER IMMIGRATION IN THE SUMMER OF 1709 TO LONDON, MUCH OF WHICH EVENTUALLY FOUND ITS WAY INTO PENNSYLVANIA.

THERE has been some discussion among historians who have dealt with the question of German immigration to America, which should be considered the first established colony. Löher[1] tells us the Spaniards, Italians, French and English may not claim the exclusive honor of founding early settlements on this continent. "In Venezuela was planted the first German colony in the New World," are his words.[2]

---

[1] Geschichte und Zustanden der Deutchen in Amerika, von Franz Löher, p. 1. This now well-established fact has also been carefully elaborated by Julius F. Sachse, Esq.

[2] Geschichte, p. 14.

The Swedish Colony. 261

The date given is 1526. The colony which settled itself on the shores of the Delaware in 1638, while ostensibly Swedish, was largely composed of Germans. Although Gustavus Adolphus and his no less illustrious minister, Axel Oxenstierna, were its promoters, the great Protestant king begged the Protestant German princes to permit their subjects to join his scheme of colonization,[3] and from the names among those colonists that have come down to us, we are assured that many of them were Germans. The charter accorded the Germans even more favorable conditions than it did to the Swedes themselves. Campanius, the earliest Swedish historian of New Sweden, tells us Germans went in the ship "der Vogel Greif" which sailed with 50 colonists to establish the first colony on the Delaware. In 1638, Peter Minnewit, the first Governor, was drowned in the West Indies. Johannes Printz, a native of Holstein, succeeded him. Although Printz was in the Swedish service, he was a German nobleman whose full name was Edler von Buchan. With Printz came 54 German families, mostly from Pomerania.[4] These facts establish the semi-German character of this so-called Swedish colony.

But when we come to look for a German colony in the New World that was distinctively such, that was permanent in its nature and left its imprint in

---

[3] Mr. Provost Stille, in Penna. Mag of Hist. and Biog.
[4] The First German Immigrants to North America, by Louis P. Hennighausen, pp. 160-162.

ineffaceable characters upon the future of the people of Pennsylvania, we must re-echo the words of the late Dr. Seidensticker who said: "Should it be asked when the German immigration in America had its beginning, the answer must be, in the year 1683."[5] He of course alludes to the Germantown settlement.

From that time forward, individuals and families found their way to the New World, but this immigration for some years was small and sporadic. We do not find that colonies of any considerable size made their way hither. In 1705 a number of German Reformed families left their homes between Wolfenbuttel and Halberstadt. They first went to Neuwied, in Rheinish Prussia, and thence to Holland, whence they sailed for New York, and finally settled in German Valley, Morris county, New Jersey.[6]

A still more important German colony was led to these shores in 1708. In January of that year, Joshua von Kocherthal, a German preacher, representing 21 families, composed of 54 persons,[7] presented himself to the resident English government agent, Davenant, at Frankfort-on-the-Main, and asked for permission to go to England, as well as for the necessary subsistence. Davenant consulted with

---

[5] "Fragt mann welcher zeit die deutsche Einwannderung in America ihren Anfang genommen habe, so lautet die Antwort: Im Jahre 1683." Bilder aus der Deutche-Pennsylvanischen Geschichte, von Oswald Seidensticker, p. 3.

[6] The Pennsylvania German Dialect, by Dr. Marion Dexter Learned.

[7] Their number is variously stated. Kapp says 61. See his Deutchen im Staate New York, p. 12.

the home government, and was advised, that no assistance could be rendered until these people received the consent of the Elector to expatriate themselves. Without more ado, Kocherthal and his little colony of Palatines, in March, made their way through the Low Countries and across the sea to London. Upon their arrival they were completely impoverished and without means of subsistence. Queen Anne allowed each a stipend of one shilling per day. What to do with them was the question. It was at first decided to send them to the island of Jamaica or Antigua, in the West Indies, but to this the Palatines objected because the climate there was so unlike their own. With their consent their destination was changed to New York, whose climate was more like that to which they were accustomed. Accordingly, on April 28, 1708, they were sent to that colony on a government vessel, accompanied by Lord Lovelace, the newly appointed Governor.[8]

---

[8] *Die Deutchen im Staate New York, während des achtzehnten Jahrhunderts*, von Freiderich Kapp. The records of the Board of Trade show that of this colony 10 were men, 10 women, 21 children, the rest unclassified. There was 1 joiner, 1 smith, and the rest were farmers, while the women understood the sams business. An effort was made to salary Kocherthal, but Secretary Boyle said he could find no authority to settle a salary on a foreign clergyman. Tools were however furnished for the colonists, and 20 pounds were given to Kocherthal for books and clothes. *See records of the Board of Trade.* Appendix B.

ARMS OF THE CITY OF LONDON.

THE GERMAN EXODUS TO ENGLAND IN 1709.

REMARKABLE MOVEMENT OF PALATINES AND SWABIANS TO LONDON, IN SEARCH OF HOMES IN THE NEW WORLD—THE MASSEN-AUSWANDERUNG OF THE GERMAN WRITERS—ATTEMPT TO TRACE ITS ORIGIN—NO SINGLE CAUSE RESPONSIBLE FOR IT.

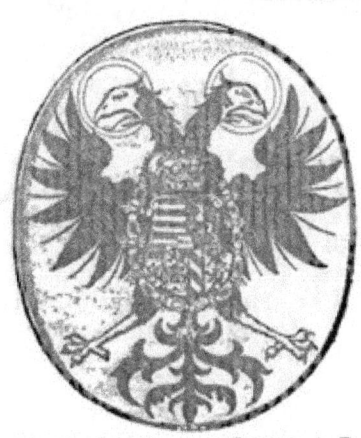

ARMS OF THE GERMAN EMPIRE, A. D. 1694.

THESE preliminary remarks bring me to the subject which it is the aim of this paper to bring into prominence, the remarkable emigration of Germans,—Palatines, Swabians and others,—to London in the spring and summer of 1709.

As has been seen, there was up to the beginning of the eighteenth century, no extended emigration movement in the direction of the English colonies in America by Germans. It is true, immigrants continued to come in the wake of the Germantown settlers, but they were either a few families at a time, or isolated individuals, and did not attract much attention. This period of comparative quietude continued uninterruptedly until 1709. During the entire period which elapsed from the establishment of the Pastorius colony in 1683 to the year 1709, the immigration was sporadic and unimportant. I have been unable to ascertain with exactness the number of Germans in Pennsylvania in the last named year, but it is almost certain that it did not exceed two or three thousand individuals, which would give us an average immigration of about 100 individuals annually during the entire period, surely a very moderate number when we consider the efforts made by Penn to secure colonists, the favorable reports sent to the old home by the Crefelders, and the wide dispersion of pamphlets throughout Germany, reciting in

---

Through the courtesy of Dr. F. D. Stone, the accomplished librarian of the Pennsylvania Historical Society, I am enabled to present to the American public this fac-simile of the letter of denization granted to the colony of Germans led to this country by the Rev. Joshua von Kocherthal, in 1708. This colony numbered fifty-four persons and was the first one composed of Germans who came across the Atlantic under the direct auspices and with the assistance of the English Government. The sum expended by the Government in planting this little colony in New York, was from first to last £655, of which amount Lord Lovelace's bill was for £202,17,8½. On August 29, 1709, Kocherthal sent a letter of thanks to the Board of Trade for its favor and kind offices. The above fac-simile, I believe, has never been printed or reproduced before.

glowing terms the advantages of Pennsylvania as a land of plenty and an asylum from oppression.

THE FIRST ARRIVALS IN LONDON.

During the months of May and June, 1709, the citizens of the city of London were astonished to find the streets of that metropolis swarming with men and women of an alien race, speaking an unknown tongue and bearing unmistakable indications of poverty, misery and want. It soon became known that about 5000 of these people were sheltered under tents in the suburbs of the city.

Additions were almost daily made to their number during June, July, August and September, and by October, between 13,000 and 14,000 had come. Then this "massen-auswanderung der Pfälzer," as Kapp calls it, gradually drew to a close.

This sudden irruption of so many thousands of foreigners within a few months, into a country where but few of them had ever appeared before, and where they were utter strangers, rather than into neighboring countries of like faith and kindred language, that would perhaps have been more ready to welcome them, stands forth as one of the most remarkable facts of the time. It was found that these people were Germans from the country lying between Landau, Spire and Mannheim, reaching almost to Cologne, commonly called the Palatinate. There were, however, many from other parts of Germany, principally from Swabia and Wurtemberg.

About the manner of their coming we learn more

Johannes Wilhelmus Elector Palatinus.

from a report made to the House of Commons in 1711, than from any other source. By that report we are told that in the spring of 1709 great numbers of these people came down the Rhine and did not pause until they reached Rotterdam, in Holland. They were even then miserably poor, and were maintained while in that city by the charity of the people. Their destination, however, was England, but for lack of the necessary shipping and want of other means, they were detained in Rotterdam. The English ministry consented to provide the necessary transportation and receive 5000 of their number.[10] Transports and other vessels were accordingly pro-

---

[10] Cassell's History of England. Text by William Howitt.

I am indebted to the courtesy of Julius F. Sachse, Esq., for the portrait of the Elector Palatine, John William, of the House of Newburg, which is here presented. I further avail myself of this opportunity to acknowledge my indebtedness to the same gentleman for other assistance both in the text and illustrations that accompany this article. His wide acquaintance with the pictorial as well as the written history of this period, freely placed at my service, has been of much value to me, and I would be doing an injustice to myself as well as to him, did I not make the fullest acknowledgement of his valuable advice and assistance.

I regret that I have been unable to supply a biography of this ruler. All I have been able to learn about him has been supplied by Protestant sources, and this, of course, has not been of a favorable character. In two lengthy letters written at that time by "A Nobleman," which I found among the papers of the late I. D. Rupp, and addressed to the English people, a long list of accusations are brought against him. The charges are mainly that he had failed to comply with the solemn treaty stipulations he had entered into with his Protestant subjects. There are no accusations of persecutions, but there were other means of manifesting his preference for his Catholic subjects. Probably he was neither better nor worse than the average petty ruler of his day.

vided by the English Government at the charge of the crown.

In one of his official communications to Mr. Secretary Boyle, Mr. Dayrolles, the English Minister at the Hague, informed that person that these immigrants were persuaded to go to England by some one in the latter country, and that even after the coming of any more had been prohibited, "a gentleman with a servant who had come over in a packet boat, had on August 20, 1709, gone to Brühl, a town near Cologne, where large numbers of Palatines were staying, and distributed money among them. Printed tickets were also sent to their friends in Germany to persuade them to do the same." Minister Dayrolles said he could never learn who this mysterious person was, much as he tried to do so. The Committee investigating the matter in England could do no more, but they did find from two letters, that one Henry Torne, a Quaker at Rotterdam, who had been acting under Minister Dayrolles, had forced a great number to embark for England after they had been provided for to return to their own country.[11]

I am strongly inclined to believe from the foregoing, that the Land Companies did not confine their efforts to secure immigration to the dissemination of booklets and other literature having that end in

---

[11] It has been suggested to me that this "unknown" may have been Benjamin Furly, an English Quaker, the life long friend of William Penn, and the promotor of the first German emigration to Pennsylvania. He was born in 1636 and died in 1714.

view, but that they were also operating through agents to persuade these people to cross the ocean and settle upon the rich and virgin lands beyond the ocean. Lord Sunderland, on May 3, 1709, said the Queen was convinced this immigration would greatly benefit her kingdom if some means could be found to settle them comfortably in England, instead of sending them to the West Indies. If, after all, the English ministry was covertly at work and instigating this exodus, they operated so secretly that their fine hand was never discovered.

In June the number sent over had reached more than ten thousand, and the Queen's Government began to be alarmed as there was no cessation, apparently, in the number clamoring to come. Secretary Boyle accordingly sent orders to her Majesty's Minister at the Hague, to prevent any further shipments until those who were already in England, should have been disposed of. To further make this fact known throughout Holland and the Palatinate, advertisements were published in the Dutch Gazettes, that no more would be carried to England. Either the pressure brought to bear on Minister Dayrolles was too strong, or his kind heart was unable to bear up under the impassionate beseechings of these friendless wanderers, so that disregarding his instructions, he sent over nearly three thousand more at Queen Anne's expense, while still others were forwarded by the charitable citizens of Rotterdam, and supplied by them with food, inasmuch as the magistrates of that place no longer permitted the immigrants even to enter the city, which of course served only to intensify their want, their sufferings and their general misery.

But neither the declarations of the English government, nor the indignation of the then Elector Palatine, John William, of the house of Newburg, who was loath to see his subjects leave him, seems to have deterred still others from making an effort to get across the North Sea. Oft repeated orders continued to be sent to the English Minister to prevent or check this exodus. Even Holland itself was appealed to, to issue similar notices, but it would seem nothing was able to stay this wholesale emigration until it had run its course, and the large number I have already mentioned had landed on the English shores. But even then it did not entirely cease. This is shown by a Proclamation or circular issued by the English government as late as the last day of December, 1709, in which further emigration is alluded to, and all persons are absolutely prohibited from coming over from Holland under pain of being immediately sent back to Germany. A fac-simile of this curious Proclamation is herewith given.[11a]

The archives of the city of Rotterdam afford us an excellent insight into the continental side of this emigration. From the records of a meeting of the Burgomasters of that city, held on April 22d, 1709, we learn it was resolved to pay to Engel Kon and Samuel de Back, four hundred and fifty guilders to be distributed among destitute families of the Lower Palatinate, for their subsistence on their journey to

Königl. Englisch in Teutschland verschickte Declaration, oder Abmahnungs-Schreiben.

Demnach letzt verwichenen Sommer/ eine grosse Anzahl armer Leuthe/ von verschiedenen Orten/ aus Teutschland allhier in Engelland angekommen/ welche bißhero von Jhrer Königlichen Majestät unterhalten / und nach und nach/ in West Jndien und nacher Jrrland versandt worden: Weilen aber dergleichen armer Leuthe seither mehr anhero gekommen / und man darauf hin nacher Holland/ und anderwerts Nachricht gegeben / daß dergleichen keine mehr passirt/ vielweniger unterhalten; die jenige auch/ welche seither dem ersten October letzhin allhier angelanget / wieder mit erster Gelegenheit / zurück über Holland nacher Teutschland gesandt werden sollen. Als wird hierdurch allen denjenigen/ welche noch intentionirt sind/ anhero zu kommen / zur Nachricht wissend gemacht /. solche ihre Reyse einzustellen /. welche gewißlich fruchtloß fallen wird/ es seydann / daß sie von selbsten bemittelt sind sich zu unterhalten. Datum Londen den 31. December 1709.

ROYAL PROCLAMATION DISTRIBUTED IN GERMANY TO DISCOURAGE FURTHER EMIGRATION TO ENGLAND.

England, and a warrant was ordered for that amount. Seven days afterwards, at another meeting of the town council it was ordered that a warrant should be drawn to pay Peter Toomen three hundred guilders to be distributed among those destitute Germans who came subsequently to those to whom money had already been paid.[12]

But the city of Rotterdam grew tired of spending so much money on these flying columns of Palatines, from whom it could expect no benefit. Accordingly on the 12th of August, 1709, the Burgomasters of the city had eight circulars prepared and distributed, in which public notice was given that the Queen of Great Britain having ordered that no more of these people should be sent over to England, until those already there had in some way been disposed of, two commissioners, Hendrick Toom and Jon van Gent, who, having out of charity taken order by direction of

---

[11a] The following is a translation of the Royal English Declaration or Proclamation (p. 271) transmitted to Germany : "Inasmuch as during the summer just past a large number of poor people arrived here in England, from different parts of Germany, who have hitherto been supported by Her Royal Majesty, and have gradually been sent to the West Indies, and afterwards to Ireland : and where as more such poor people have come hither since, notice has consequently been sent to Holland and elsewhere that none such would be passed much less supported, and that those also, who have arrived here since the first of last October were to be sent back to Germany via Holland at the first opportunity. All such as intend to come hither are therefore notified to desist from their voyage which would assuredly result in failure unless it be that they have means of their own with which to support themselves. Dated, London, the 31st of December, 1709."

[12] See Appendix "A" for full detail, quoted from the minutes of the proceedings of the City Council of Rotterdam.

her Majesty to provide transportation and other necessities for these people, should also be instructed to notify all persons who might yet intend to come from Germany, to remain away and prevent them making a fruitless journey.

The two agents just named were instructed to put two yachts on the rivers Waal and Maas and cruise on those streams in order to turn back any emigrants who might be coming down on their way to Rotterdam and England. It was stated that they had already stopped one thousand and turned them back. The council on August 24, allowed them three hundred and fifty guilders for their services. The Burgomasters of the city of Brielle, a fortified town in South Holland, also adopted a scheme to shift the burden of supporting some of these people from their own shoulders. They wrote a letter to the Rotterdam authorities stating many Germans were there on their way to Rotterdam in a starving condition, and asked assistance to help support them, they being unable to do so by themselves. In a long and very polite letter dated on the 26th of August, the Rotterdammers replied, and went into the details of what they had already done for those who had come among them, and how they had at great expense adopted precautions to prevent the arrival of any more. They told the Brielle people that but for these precautions, the general situation would be still worse.

On September 16th, 1709, the Burgomasters of Rotterdam again met in council, and a letter from the English Minister Dayrolles was read, in which he requested that the city should order that no more Germans should be sent or allowed to go to England. The wily Hollanders in reply made answer that "they could not prevent those families of the Palatines who were already in this country in order to go to England, from being taken thither, but that the Minister at Cologne and Frankfurt should be ordered to warn the people over there not to come this way for that purpose," and that is all the satisfaction Minister Dayrolles got. Finally, the city of Rotterdam prohibited all these emigrants from coming into that place.

It does not appear from any of the records that the Holland Government itself made any appropriations for the maintenance of these people while in that country, but left that duty upon the shoulders of the several municipalities themselves and to the charity of the people at large. No doubt it proved as grievous a burden there, as it did in England when they reached that country. From all the evidence, it appears that the English government was in every case compelled to pay the cost of transportation from Holland to London.

Most opportunely, through the liberality of the Pennsylvania Historical Society, new and original records have been thrown open to our inspection and use, in a copy of the original Board of Trade Journals which that Society has had made, and in which are recorded the " Proceedings of her Majesty's Commissioners for promoting the trade of this Kingdom

Action of the Board of Trade.

and for inspecting and improving her Plantations in America and elsewhere." The notice of the Commissioners was first called to this question by a letter from the Earl of Sunderland, on May 4, 1709, who was Secretary of State at the time, who stated that some hundreds of poor German Protestants had lately arrived, that more were coming, and asking the Board to consider the best means of settling them in some part of the kingdom.

In all, I find that the Board met about twenty times to consider the various phases presented by the German exodus. All the action that was taken by the Government seems to have been inspired by the discussions and investigations of the Commissioners. The task before the Commissioners was a troublesome one and took up much of their time during the summer of 1709.[12a]

[12a] See Appendix B.

CAUSES LEADING TO THE EXODUS.

THE QUESTION OF PERSECUTION EXAMINED—ENGLAND'S SHARE IN THE WORK—THE COLD WINTER OF 1708-1709—OPERATIONS OF THE LAND COMPANIES—PENN'S INVITATIONS—LETTERS FROM PENNSYLVANIA AND BOOKLETS.

ROYAL ARMS OF HOLLAND.

SO remarkable was this Palatine emigration that historians have endeavored to discover some great moving cause, some all powerful impulse to which they might ascribe it. They have not found it for it did not exist. After going over the ground carefully, however, I have had no difficulty in reaching very convincing and satisfactory conclusions.

No single cause was responsible for this wonderful exodus of a people from their firesides, who, perhaps, beyond all others, are most strongly attached to home and country. There was probably since the fall of the Roman Empire, no period of greater unrest in Europe than the closing years of the seventeenth and the opening years of the eighteenth century. The ceaseless disturber of the world's peace, the arch plotter of Europe was still alive, and although past seventy years of age, Louis XIV continued to keep almost every country within his reach, embroiled in foreign or domestic strife. For forty years he had been almost continuously at war with foreign powers. The war of the Spanish succession was now on. Spain, Italy, Germany and the Netherlands echoed to the tramp of desolating armies. Peter the Great and his allies, the kings of Denmark and Poland, were struggling with Charles XII of Sweden, and the contest convulsed the North and East of Europe for more than twenty years.

Germany had for many years been the battle field of Europe. The soldiers of almost every nation had in turn trampled on her soil and despoiled her people. The Palatinate, bordering both on France and Germany had been the provinces most subject to invasion and spoliation. Surely, this dreadful condition of things was in itself enough to induce these miserable people to forsake the land of their birth by thousands.

RELIGIOUS PERSECUTIONS.

So far as I have been able to learn there were at this time no direct religious persecutions; the testimony on this point is concurrent and conclusive. But there were men still living who remembered the days of old; whose friends and relatives had passed through the tortures of the stake and the fagot, and who would carry those memories to their dying day. There are extant two long letters,[13] written in 1698, in which the religious condition of the Protestant Palatines is fully described. They give in detail the broken promises and petty persecutions of the Elector. How the treaty of Munster was shamelessly ignored. We know that religious motives sent the Puritans and the Quakers to the New World, and this had also much to do in setting on foot the Teutonic emigration that turned towards Pennsylvania. By the treaty of Westphalia, only three confessions were tolerated in Germany: the Catholic, Reformed and Lutheran. The " sect " people passed under the yoke.[14] It was that which sent the Mennonites, the Schwenckfelders and the Mystics of Ephrata and the Wissahicon to Pennsylvania. This fact crops out on every page of their history. Whenever contemporary authorities deal with this German exodus, the religious aspect of the case is invariably introduced and frequently is the only one alluded to. We must not forget, however, that whether the emigrants left the Fatherland in larger or smaller numbers, there were nearly always some Catholics among them. In the great migration under consideration

---

[13] "A true account of the sad condition of the Protestants in the Palatinate, in 1698, in two letters to an English gentleman." These letters were originally printed in London in 1699, by Richard Parker.

[14] Seidensticker.

THE PENNSYLVANIA-GERMAN SOCIETY.

the Catholics were quite numerous. Many of these who refused to embrace the Protestant religion, were sent back to the Palatinate where the ruling house, as well as the ruling prince, as has already been said, were both Catholic. While, therefore, the questions of persecution and religious motives are to be considered, they were by no means the only, not even the principal ones. It is true that in a memorial which was issued in their behalf in London, there are allusions to persecutions, but these occurred full twenty years before.

The Elector, John William, seems to have been stung by the oft-repeated charge of having persecuted his Protestant subject, and in consequence, the Protestant Consistory of the Palatinate, by his direction, issued and spread throughout Britain, Holland and Germany, the following declaration:

"Good Queen Anne," as her own and succeeding generations have delighted to call her. Queen of Great Britain and the last sovereign of the House of Stuart, was born on Feb. 6th, 1665. She was the daughter of the Duke of York, afterwards James II of England, and VII of Scotland. Although her father embraced the Catholic religion, Anne, who had been educated in the Protestant faith, always retained an ardent affection for it. She married Prince George of Denmark in 1683, an indolent but good natured sort of a man. On the death of William III, she succeeded to the crown. During the earlier part of her reign, she was largely under the influence of the Duke of Marlborough and his scheming wife, and this was manifested in much of her public career. Party strife ran high and political combinations made her reign a turbulent one. The successes of that great Captain, the Duke of Marlboroughs made her reign a continual scene of public glory. The Union of Scotland with the British crown was consummated while she occupied the throne. So many eminent men in literature and science flourished at this time, that her's has been called the Augustan age of Britain.

A Translation from the High-Dutch, *of a Declaration made (by Direction from the* Elector Palatine) *by the Protestant Consistory in the* Palatinate.

"Whereas it has been signify'd to the Reform'd Consistory in the *Palatinate*, that several of the Families, who are gone down the *Rhine*, to proceed to *Pensilvania*, to settle themselves there, commonly pretend they are oblig'd to retire thither for the Sake of Religion, and the Persecution which they suffer upon that Account; and since it is not known to any of the Consistory, that those with-drawn Subjects have complain'd, that they suffer'd at that Time any Persecution on Account of Religion, or that they were forc'd to quit their Country for want of Liberty of Conscience, contrary to his Electoral Highness's gracious Declaration of the 21st of *November*, 1705. therefore, as soon as the Consistory understood that a Number of Subjects were gone out Abroad to the said *Pensilvania*, and that more were like to follow, they thought it necessary to acquaint all the reform'd Inspectors and Ministers with it, to undeceive their Auditors, as also these withdrawn People, and that they are not like to gain their End in all Probability, and to perswade them against their withdrawing any farther; as also to the Intent to shew the groundless Pretences of such People to go out of the Country on Account of the said Religious Persecution. Which we do attest hereby in favour of Truth.

"Done at *Heidleburg* the 27th of *June*, 1709.

"L. S. The Vice-President and Council of the Consistory constituted in the Electoral *Palatinate*.

"*V. P. Howmuller, T. Heyles, H. Crontz, J. Closter. Z. Kirchmejer. Schemel.*

The Edict of Nantes. 281

If it were possible to ascertain with fullness and certainty, the extent to which Queen Anne and her government were responsible for this movement, I am fully satisfied we had about reached the true solution. England retained a lively remembrance of the results that followed the revocation of the Edict of Nantes. That unwise act sent 700,000 of France's best citizens to Germany, Switzerland, Holland and Britain. They were largely handicraftsmen and carried their various manufacturing industries, their skill and their industry with them, giving thereby a wonderful impulse to industrial trades wherever they went. The long and costly wars England had carried on, took away many of her people and this was felt to be a most serious drawback to national prosperity. It was desirable to replace them with the unsatisfied people of Germany, who were known to be skillful in many trades, as well as reliable and thrifty.

I have found a number of references to a proclamation by the Queen, said to favor, if not actually invite, these people to come to England.[14a] A careful

---

Queen Anne was too much swayed by her ministers and favorites to be called a great Queen, but as a woman she deserves our admiration. She was a sincere friend of the Palatines, doing everything in her power to improve their condition while in England, and to settle them comfortably elsewhere. She was of medium size, comely, but not beautiful. If she was not great as a queen, never was there a more virtuous, affectionate and conscientious a woman or one more worthy of esteem. Our portrait is a reproduction from the famous one of Sir Godfrey Kneller.

[14a] ' On a proclamation of Queen Anne, of England, 1708, some three

examination of all the authorities that were accessible to me, shows no evidence sustaining this allegation. There is no reason to suspect her of even having authorized the famous "Golden Book," so largely circulated in Germany, containing a portrait of herself, with the title printed in gold. That she was throughout these trying times the sincere friend of these immigrants, there is no room to doubt. We are told in Luttrell's diary that in response to a letter from the King of Prussia, she declared she had already given her ministers abroad, instructions to aid the French Protestants and would further aid them as far as lay in her power. The fact is that her treatment of them while in England was everything that could reasonably be expected of her, and that she even sent assistance to those in Holland, clearly shows that the earnest sympathies of the warm hearted Queen were thoroughly aroused in the cause of these homeless wanderers. If any proclamation had been issued by her, it would surely be in

---

or four thousand Germans went in 1709, to Holland, and were thence transported to England." Rupp's Hist. Lancaster county, p. 182.

Löehr says: Da verzweifelten viele am Leben, *und als die Einladung der englischen Königin Anna*, eine freie Überfahrt nach Amerika, und gutes Land umsonst zu gewinnen, den Rhein entlang verkundigt wurde, brach man in Masse auf, und es begab sich jener Zug der mehr als dreissig tausand Deutchen, welcher ein Denkmal ist des deutchen Elends." *Die Deutchen in Amerika, p. 42.*

Rupp evidently followed Löehr blindly as others have done since. If these writers have any evidence of what they assert why have they not produced it, or indicated chapter and verse where it may be found? I reiterate therefore that I am fully persuaded the story is a mere figment of the imagination, having its origin in the Queen's well-known kindly attitude towards these people.

Drawn by J. Thurston. Engraved by R.Rivers.

SIDNEY GODOLPHIN.
Lord High Treasurer of Great Britain from 1702 until 1710.

From a Drawing by Bulfinch in the Collection at Strawberry Hill.

evidence somewhere. But even the inquiry instigated by the House of Commons as to the causes of this influx of Palatines, and undertaken by an opposite administration, failed to reveal anything of the kind. Surely if there had been such a thing, it would have been discovered. I am fully satisfied therefore, that no such document was ever issued, either by the Government or by the Queen. It was simply one way of accounting for a perplexing condition of things.[14b]

THE COLD WINTER OF 1708-9.

I am inclined to believe that a most potent cause in bringing about this remarkable migration was the cold winter of 1708-9. All the contemporary author-

---

[14b] The Ministry at this period was Whig. Charles Spencer, Earl of Sunderland was Secretary of State, from 1706 until 1710; and Sidney, Earl of Godolphin, was Lord High Treasurer, from 1702 until 1710. In the latter year, however, there was a change in the political complexion of the country. The Tories came into power, with Henry St. John, Viscount Bolingbroke, as Foreign Secretary, and Robert Harley, Earl of Oxford, as Chancellor of the Exchequer. The German immigration having been most distasteful to the majority of the English people, especially the lower classes, the new Ministry at once proceeded to make itself popular by beginning an inquiry into the causes of the coming of so many thousands of these people. A parliamentary committee consisting of sixty-nine members of the House was appointed to make a searching investigation "upon what invitation or encouragement the Palatines came over and what moneys were expended in bringing them into Great Britain, and for maintaining them here, and by whom paid," but nothing was discovered incriminating the former administration, or connecting the Queen with the movement except in a way to do her exceeding honor. This investigation was a fortunate thing, inasmuch as it has made us acquainted with much concerning this movement which otherwise might never have been disclosed.

ities are agreed as to its unexampled severity. It was general throughout Western Europe, but especially was it felt among the starving citizens of the Palatinate, whose lands and homes had so long and so often been despoiled by persecutions and wars. The pen almost refuses to do its task when asked to tell of the hundreds of strong men who, during that memorable winter, lay down to die of cold and hunger in the once fruitful valley of the Rhine. So intense was the cold that even the wild animals of the forest and the birds of the air were frozen to death. Wine was frozen in the casks and bottles. The vineyards were frozen to the ground and the fruit trees completely destroyed.[15]

Tindal refers to the intense frost of that winter. He says: "The severity of the winter season was very remarkable this year, (1708-9), for it began to freeze the night before Christmas Day, with great violence, and not long after fell great snows. Those who compared the great frost of 1683-4 with this, observed that the first was generally a bright one, and continued about two months without interruption; but the latter mostly dark, with some intervals lasted a month longer; during which many cattle, especially sheep, and likewise birds, perished. The Thames was frozen over, and on the 3rd of January, people began to erect booths and set up tents on the ice. This occasioned a thin harvest and

---

[15] See Löehr, who says: "Endlich kam der gräszliche Winter von 1709, hinzu, wo die Vögel in der Luft und das Wild in den Wäldern erfroren und die Menchen verhungerten. Page 42.

this a scarcity of corn. This great frost was general in Europe, but most severely felt in France, where in most places the fruit trees were killed, and the corn frozen to the ground, which occasioned there a dreadful calamity and desolation."[16]

Need we wonder, therefore, that these wretched people, who had previously undergone so much from the invasions of contending armies, were at length driven to despair by this terrible visitation of the forces of nature? Where armies were no longer able to collect resources, what hope was there for the individual citizen? Their heart-rending lamentations filled the listening air and existence seemed only possible in another clime and under new conditions. To make matters worse, even in that time of dire distress, speculators came to the front, bought the grain that frugal farmers had saved and sought to make a profit even out of famine. Nor could all the efforts on the part of the government check it. An eye witness says of the financial situation: "Nobody could pay any more, because nobody was paid. The people of the country in consequence of exactions had become insolvent; commerce dried up and brought no returns. Good faith and confidence were abolished." Chaos, ruin and universal suffering prevailed.

I come now to what, after all, may be ascribed the principal cause leading up to this extraordinary

---

[16] Tindal's History of England, Book xxvi. See also James' History of Louis XIV.

movement. William Penn had made two visits to Germany, one in 1671 and the second in 1677. At that time he had not yet acquired the Province that was to make his name so memorable. But he became well known through the peculiar religious tenets he advocated and attempted to spread. Later, when the owner of Pennsylvania, he spared no efforts to attract colonists from Germany. Not only did he write full descriptions of the Province where lands were almost given away, but political and religious toleration was proclaimed as the very corner stone of his new government. Many of these attractively written brochures are still extant to show us how great were the efforts to arouse the spirit of emigration.

Then, too, the spirit of speculation stepped in and did much to forward the project. One company after another was formed to arouse and encourage the migrating impulse. The West India Company, The Frankford Company and many more were engaged in this work. Seidensticker tells us that the latter company is directly attributable to Penn. He also asserts that Penn gave the first impulse to this German exodus.[17] Bancroft bears testimony to the same effect.[18] The climate, resources and general advantages of Penn's Province were well known all over Germany.

It is true that more than a generation had passed

---

[17] Der anstosz zur deutchen Auswanderung im eigentlichen Sinne ging von William Penn aus. Bilder, p. 4.

Groß-Brittannisches AMERICA

Nach seiner
Erfindung/Bevölckerung
und
Allerneuestem Zustand.

Terre-Neuf.	St. Lucia.
Neu-Schottland.	St. Vincent.
Neu-Engelland.	Dominico.
Neu-Yorck.	Antego.
Neu-Jersey.	Montserrat.
Pensylvanien.	Nevis.
Maryland.	Barbuda.
Virginien.	Anguilla.
Carolina.	Jamaica.
Hudsons-Bay.	Bahama/ und
Barbados.	Bermudas.

Aus dem Englischen übersetzet
durch
M. Vischer.

Hamburg/ in Verlegung Zacharias Hertels
Buchhändlers im Dohm/ 1710.

TITLE PAGE OF GERMAN EDITION OF OLDMIXON'S BRITISH AMERICA.

by since the gentle Quaker's, visit to the Rhine provinces, and many of those who had met him face to face were no longer among the living. But there were still some there who had seen and heard him. A new series of publications also began to appear about the year 1700, and these were widely distributed all over Germany and the Low Countries. Once more the tales of a land flowing with milk and honey were told; a land where the climate was more temperate than in Germany; where the conditions of life were most desirable; where all creeds were tolerated; where kings and priestcraft were unknown; where universal freedom prevailed; where strife never came; where not only ease and comfort but certain wealth awaited the industrious settlers:—this and much more was heard around every fireside and fell like the voice of enchantment upon the ears of the harried and starving Palatines. There was also an old German prophecy to the effect that in America they would prosper and be happy.[19] With all these things continually pressed upon their attention, and with the grim spectre of spoliations, hardships, intolerance and want rising gloomily out of the past, need we seek further, need we even wonder, that

---

[18] "Meanwhile the news spread abroad that William Penn, the Quaker, had opened 'an asylum to the good and the oppressed of every nation,' and humanity went through Europe, gathering the children of misfortune. From England and Wales, from Scotland and Ireland and the Low Countries emigrants crowded to the land of promise."
Bancroft's United States, vol. 2, p. 391.

[19] E. K. Martin. The Mennonites.

entire communities uprose as one man, shook the dust of the Fatherland from their feet—that Fatherland so dear to the German heart—and with little or no preparation, took flight for a land where their lives should thereafter be passed in plenty and in peace?

Another cause and by no means an unimportant one must also be mentioned. The colonists who had come to Pennsylvania prior to 1709, were, with very few exceptions, satisfied with the condition of things as they found them. The Germantown colony itself was in the land business, and therefore interested in bringing over as many colonists as possible. Selfish motives may have moved the people of Germantown equally with their desire to benefit their countrymen, but whatever the motive, it turned the expectant eyes and the waiting footsteps towards the New World.

BRITAIN'S NATURALIZATION ACT.

Still another cause remains to be mentioned. For twenty years the passage of a general naturalization law for Protestant foreigners coming into, or residing in the Kingdom, conditioned on their taking the oaths and communing in the English church, had been discussed in the newspapers and by pamphleteers. Up to this time Holland had drawn to herself most of the German Protestants who had emigrated from Catholic states, enriching that country by their industries and their thrift. Englishmen were anxious to turn at least a portion of these people across the channel. This eventually led to the passage of the naturalization law.[20] Luttrell thought this matter so important that he gave it close attention in his diary as the following will show:

Saturday, Feb. 5, 1709. The Commons this day gave leave to bring in a bill for naturalizing all foreign protestants.

Thursday, Feb. 24. This day a second time the bill for naturalizing foreign protestants, and committed it for Monday.

Tuesday, 1 March. Yesterday the Commons in a Committee, went through the bill for naturalizing foreign protestants, and to be repeated to-morrow.

Thursday, 3 March. The Commons ordered the bill for naturalizing foreign protestants to be engrost.

Thursday, March 24. Yesterday the Lords Commissioners appointed by her Majesty, sent for the Commons to come up to the House of Peers, and gave the royal assent to the bill for naturalizing protestants.

Saturday, 14 May. A great many poor German and French protestants have taken the oaths this

---

[20] An extract from the oath which these naturalized foreigners were compelled to take, is here given:

Ich, A. B. schwere, dass ich von ganzem Herzen verabscheue und abschwere, als gottlos und ketzerisch, die verdammte Lehre und Satz, dass Fürsten, welche der PAPST, oder der Romische Stuhl, hat in Bann gethan, können von ihren Unterthanen, oder sonst jemanden, abgesetzt und ermordet werden. Und ich bekenne, dass kein ausländischer Fürst, Person, Prälat, Stand order Potentat habe, oder soll haben, einige Jurisdiction, Gewalt, Oberherrschaft, Vorzug, oder Autorität in Geistlichen und Kirchen-Sachen in diesem Königreich. So helfe mir Gott.

CHARLES Earl of SUNDERLAND.

Secretary of State of Great Britain from 1706 until 1710.

Immigration Attributed to the Act. 291

week at the Queen's Bench Court, in order to their naturalization by the late act.[20a]

While the act was passed about the time the first emigrants began to arrive, and would therefore not seem to have been an inducing cause, yet the concurrent testimony of a number of authorities on this point seems nevertheless to give color to this fact.

One authority say: "In consequence of the naturalization act, there came over in May, 7000 of the poor Palatines and Swabians, who had been utterly ruined and driven from their habitations by the French.[21] Dick Steele, when the immigration had set in, said in the *Tatler:* " Our late act of naturalization hath had so great effect in foreign parts, that some princes have prohibited the French refugees in their dominions to sell or transfer their estates to any other of their subjects; and at the same time have granted them greater immunities than they hitherto enjoyed. It has been also thought necessary to restrain their own subjects from leaving their country on pain of death.[22] The latter clause no doubt refers to the Elector Palatine himself, as Luttrell under date of April 28, says: " Foreign letters advise that the Elector Palatine, upon many families leaving his dominions and gone to England to be transported to Pennsylvania, has published an order making it death and confiscation of goods, for any of his sub-

---

[20a] A Brief Historical Relation of State Affairs from Sept. 1678 to April, 1714. By Narcissus Luttrell, Oxford, 1857. 6 vols.

[21] Anderson's History of England.

[22] Tatler, No. 13, May, 1709.

jects to quit their native countries."[23] It must be confessed, that cause and effect in this case seem to follow each other very closely, but no doubt it was well known that the law would be passed and men made ready in anticipation. Holland, too, seems to have thought the act had something to do with the great outgoing of the people, as on the 24th of June, just three months after the English law was promulgated, the States General issued a proclamation, offering to naturalize all the refugees from France and other countries who had sought a domicile in Holland, and confer on them and all other worthy persons who might hereafter come, all the privileges of citizenship.[23a]

While various accounts, among them those set forth by the Palatines themselves after they arrived in England, give various reasons for this extraordinary movement, yet through them all runs one long, unvarying refrain—the hope of bettering themselves, of securing religious toleration and domestic tranquillity. I say again, therefore, as I have already said, that no one reason or cause was responsible for this remarkable movement, but that it was the result of a combination of causes, which had long been at work, and which at length made themselves seen and felt in the manner here set forth.

---

[23] Luttrell's Diary.
[23a] See Appendix D.

THE STAY IN ENGLAND.

MAINTAINED BY GOVERNMENT AID AND BY PRIVATE SUB-
SCRIPTIONS—VARIOUS PROJECTS FOR THEIR SETTLEMENT—
SCATTERED IN ALL PARTS OF THE KINGDOM—UNHAPPY
CONDITION AND THEIR APPEAL TO THE PUBLIC—INCIDENTS
OF THEIR LIFE IN LONDON.

Arms of Penn.

WE now come to the long stay of these Palatines in London and the surrounding country, a stay that was not more agreeable to them than it was unwelcome to the English. Never before, perhaps, were emigrants seeking new homes in a distant land, so poorly provided with money and the other necessaries of life to support them on their way, as were these Palatines. All contemporary accounts agree on this point and there is besides abundant evidence to sustain them.

Ships had to be provided by the English government to bring them from Rotterdam. From the day of their arrival in London they required the assistance of the English to keep them from starving. There was little or no work; bread was dear, and the only thing to do was to bridge the crisis by raising money by public subscriptions. On June 7, 1709, the Justices of the Peace for the county of Middlesex, sent a petition to the Queen, asking for authority to take up collections in their behalf in all the churches, as well as from the public generally, throughout the county. The Queen not only granted the desired authority, but on June 16, in Council, she being present, orders were prepared and a Brief was issued at once. This Brief was soon thereafter made to extend to the entire kingdom, including Scotland and Wales, the need having grown from day to day, and the charge on the crown having become a burden. In this paper recital was made of the many hardships these people had suffered in their own country during the previous years, and it was ordered that collections should be lifted in all the churches, and that the curates and wardens should proceed from house to house, asking for contributions which were to be distributed among the needy Palatines through a Royal Commission, which included the Archbishop of Canterbury, the Lord High Chancellor, the Dukes of Devonshire, Newcastle, Somerset, Ormond, Bedford, and Buckingham, besides many of the most eminent persons among the gentry.[24]

The well known Bishop Burnet, who throughout these troublesome times was the staunch friend of the Palatines, at the same time sent out a circular letter to the clergy of his diocese, asking their earnest efforts to stir up the people to be liberal in this charity. The result of these efforts was that the large sum of £19,838.11 was collected and distributed to relieve their necessities. Considering the difference in the value of money between that period and the present time, it must be admitted the Englishmen were liberal, especially when we remember how long wars, and the payment of subsidies to other nations, absorbed the money of the English nation. At that very hour, the King of Denmark, the King of Portugal, the Duke of Savoy, the King of Prussia, the Landgrave of Hesse Cassel, the Elector of Treves and the Elector Palatine were all heavily subsidized by the English Government, on account of the war then carried on.

But while food was thus provided, shelter was also needed. The Queen directed that a thousand tents be taken out of the Tower of London for their use. But of course these were far from sufficient, and for a time even no suitable place to pitch them could be found. Eventually, part were set up on Blackheath,[25]

---

[24] In Appendix C will be found the full text of the petition sent to the Queen by the Justices of the Peace for the county of Middlesex, as well as the "Brief" issued by the Queen in response to the same. A full list of the persons who were appointed to superintend these collections is also appended as a matter of historic interest. One hundred persons were engaged in the work.

[25] Blackheath was a large, elevated, open common in the county of Kent, seven miles south-east of London. Once it was of considerable size but it has been encroached upon to such an extent that at present it

on the south side of the Thames, near Greenwich, and the rest at Camberwell.[26] Some found lodgings in private houses; others were permitted to occupy barns until harvest time, when, of course they would be required to house the crops. Sir Charles Cox gave up his large warehouse, although desired by the parish officers not to do so, for fear of the expense and of probable infection. He offered it for two

---

comprises only about 70 acres. For several hundred years it has been a favorite holiday resort of the citizens of London. The inimitable diarist Samuel Pepys, speaks of having gone there in 1665 to test a carriage fitted with springs, a new invention, it would seem. This high-lying spot was also a favorite military camping ground. John Evelyn says, under date of June 10, 1673, 'we went, after dinner, to see the formal and formidable camp on Blackheath, raised to invade Holland; or, as others suspected, for another design." In 1683 he visited the same spot to see "the new fair," it pretended to be for the sale of cattle he tells us, but adds, "There appeared nothing but an innumerable assembly of people from London, peddlers, &c." Again in 1685 he was there to see six Scotch and English regiments encamped there, about to return to Holland : "The King and Queen came to see them exercise." The last visit he records was made on July 20, 1690, on which day, "a camp of about 4,000 men was begun to be formed on Blackheath."

Blackheath is also noted for being the scene of some of the most important occurrences in the English history. The peasant revolt under Wat Tyler originated there. Jack Cade, the leader of the insurrection of 1450, when he marched on London with upwards of 15,000 adherents, encamped on this historic spot. The revolutionary Cornishmen under Lord Audley in 1497 also made it their stopping place. The Danes, at the time of their invasion of Britain, in 1011, encamped here. To this renowned place flocked all London to welcome Henry V. upon his return to England after winning the glorious field of Agincourt. Here also, Charles II, on his way from Dover met the army of the Restoration. Blackheath, even so late as the closing years of the eighteenth century was a famous resort of highwaymen and some of the most notorious cutpurses in England's criminal annals made it the scene of their exploits. [See Evelyn's Diary: Chambers Encyclopædia, etc.]

[26] Camberwell was, and is a parish and suburb of London, in the county of Surry, distant about two miles from St. Paul's Cathedral.

months without rent, but conditioned that if they remained longer he was to be paid for the entire time. He was paid 100 guineas to allow them to remain until they were sent to Ireland and elsewhere. He received that sum on Feb. 9, 1710. Fourteen hundred were lodged there.

Meanwhile the Board of Trade, which had the general supervision of the whole business, was not idle. The records of this Board, which have been rendered accessible during the past few months in this country, give ample testimony to the trouble and anxiety these people were causing the Government.[26a] It met almost daily in the palace of Whitehall and from the proceedings we get a clear idea of what was done to support and establish them.[27]

[26a] See Appendix B.

[27] The historian, Macaulay, calls Whitehall "the most celebrated palace in which the English sovereigns have ever dwelt." It once occupied an area of great extent, fronting the Thames on the east, St James Park on the west and stretching from Scotland Yard on the north to Cannon-row on the south. If the walls of this venerable structure could record the sayings and doings they have heard and witnessed, the chronicle would almost fill up the mediæval history of England. From the days of the Tudors to those of the Stuarts, the names of the most illustrious personages in the history of the empire have been closely associated with this famous place

Its original name was York House, so named by Cardinal Wolsey, who once lived in it, but when that proud prelate lost the favor of his Sovereign, it was surrendered to the crown, when it received its present name. It was the palace of the Kings of England from the reign of Henry VIII, to William III. There was at one time a thoroughfare through it to St. Margaret's cemetery which offended King Henry VIII, so he opened a new burying ground at St. Martin's-in-the-Fields. In front of the banqueting hall of the palace, on January 30, 1649, was enacted one of the darkest scenes in all English history, the execution on the scaffold of Charles I.

WHITEHALL PALACE.

Several times it was proposed to locate them in different parts of the kingdom itself. They called to their assistance the Lutheran and Reformed clergymen in London, three in number, at the time, who it seems were located in the Savoy district,[28] and

In addition to being the Royal residence, Whitehall was also the place where all the public officials of the Kingdom had their offices. The Treasury, the offices of the Privy Council, of the Secretary of State, of the Lords of the Board of Trade, and indeed all the important public departments were located here. It was in the rooms of the Board of Commissioners for the Colonies that all the discussions concerning the Palatines were carried on, as will be seen by a reference to Appendix B. It is this fact that gives us a direct interest in this famous building and has led me to introduce a pictorial illustration of it in this connection.

On January 4, 1698, a most disastrous fire broke out in the Palace lasting all night, and by morning some of the most notable parts of the structure had been swept away. Many masterpieces of art and other treasures were destroyed. Macaulay devotes several pages in Chap. xxiii of his History to this occurrence

[28] The "SAVOY" is a well known district in London. The "Savoy Palace" was built here by Peter of Savoy in the first part of the XIV century. It was the scene of many stirring events in English history. It was destroyed by Wat Tyler and his fellow rebels in 1381. Henry VII rebuilt it and endowed it as a hospital King Charles I established a French church there. Fleetwood describes it in 1581 as "the chief nurserie of evil people, rogues and masterless men," it having become a refuge for poor debtors when fleeing from their creditors. The *London Postman* of 1696 says "a person going into the Savoy to collect a debt due him was seized by the inhabitants and according to usual custom, dipped in tar and rolled in feathers." In 1661 the Commission appointed to revise the Book of Common Prayer met here, and was known as the Savoy Conference.

In 1694 a German Lutheran congregation was established in the Savoy district and met in the Savoy chapel. It is this church, known as St. Mary's of Savoy and the clergymen who ministered therein in 1709 to which allusion is made above. At this period there seem to have been three clergymen there; George Andreas Ruperti Mr. Tribekko and (perhaps) Mr. Treke. These were the persons who seem also to have had general charge of the newly arrived Germans. It was here that their spiritual

THE SAVOY PALACE AND CHAPEL.

these, from time to time, every few days in fact, made reports of the numbers of the Palatines, their con-

---

home was and here the ministrations of the church were given them. Here the sacraments were administered and here, when they died, as many hundreds did, the last rites were performed and they were laid to rest in the burial ground belonging to the church. It is a "God's acre" to which the men of German blood, wherever they may be, will always turn with feelings of profound interest and reverence.

A German Reformed congregation was also established within the bounds of the Savoy district, about the year 1697. One of its earliest pastors was the Rev. Planta, who was also the Chief Librarian of the British Museum, and Secretary of the Royal Academy of Sciences. A few years later the Congregation was in charge of the Rev. Dr. Gottfried Woide, who also became Chief Librarian of the British Museum.

dition, needs, and occupations.[29] It was stated that most of the men were husbandmen, and many of the rest handcraftsmen, while the women could spin and knit. The first 852 were allowed £20 per day. It was also proposed that they be granted parcels of land in her Majesty's forests and chases in order to convert them to tillage. A proposition was also received from the Society of London for Mines Royal, proposing the employment of the strongest in the silver and copper mines of Penlyn and Merionethshire. A project for settling some of them in Staffordshire and Gloucestershire, proposed by Lord Chamberlain, was also considered. Eventually it was found this would entail a cost of £150,000 and it was abandoned. It was suggested to employ some of them in the mines of Wales. It was agreed, however, to give special encouragement to persons and parishes who should be willing to receive them, and the sum of £5 was offered per head, the Queen to be at the charge of sending them to their respective places.

Still the allowance of the government was insufficient to properly sustain these people, and they were obliged to beg for bread on the streets of London, and this begging was principally done by the married women.

A contemporary publication in summing up these events said: "Some well meaning but perhaps not sufficiently thoughtful persons, touched by the suffer-

---
[29] See Appendix B.

KIRCHEN-ORDNUNG,

Der Chriſtlichen und der ungeänderten
Augſpurgiſchen Confeſſion
Zugethanen
Gemeinde in LONDON,
Welche,
Durch Gottliche Verleyhung,
Im 1694. Jahre,

Am 19ten Sonntage nach dem Feſt der Heiligen Dreyfaltigkeit,

Solenniter Eingeweyhet und Eingeſegnet worden,

In St. Mary's Savoy.

Ep. 1. Cor. 14. v. 33. 40.

GOTT iſt nicht ein GOTT der Unordnung, ſondern des Friedens, wie in allen Gemeinen der Heiligen. Laſſe es alles ehrlich und ordentlich zugehen.

Rom. 15. v. 33.

Der GOTT des Friedens ſey mit euch allen! Amen.

TITLE PAGE OF PRAYER-BOOK OF THE GERMAN SAVOY
CONGREGATION IN LONDON. USED IN
PENNSYLVANIA PRIOR TO 1748.

ings of the Palatines, ruined through long wars and heavy taxes, had allowed themselves to be informed that these people could be better cared for in England if they betook themselves thither, and from thence to places to be indicated. This resulted in a great uprising in the Palatinate and the adjoining regions, so that the people hastened to England in great numbers, hoping to find there long desired happiness and abundance of food, and in a short time many thousands reached English soil, so that in May, 6520 persons had arrived. It had been the intention to provide for all of these in the Province of Kent, negotiations had been begun to purchase the large forest and zoological garden at Coloham, belonging to Sir Joseph Williamson, and which had been offered for sale, but he declined to sell it although offered its full value according to the estimates of the day. Meanwhile the poor people lay there and more were almost daily added to their number. Germany was notified that no more could be received, and several hundred Catholics were sent back with alms, because they could not be allowed to remain under the laws of the realm. For the remainder huts were built and a number of dwelling places in Hampshire allotted them to live in. One hundred commissioners,[30] representing all ranks and conditions, were appointed, among them dukes, margraves, earls, bishops and others, and a collection throughout the entire kingdom was permitted for

---

[30] For complete list of the names see Appendix C.

their benefit, which must have produced a large sum, because some persons contributed 500 thalers and others even 1000, and the Queen herself ordered a daily distribution of 800 thalers among them, and also gave them 1000 High-German Bibles."[31]

From the beginning they were objects of dislike by the poorer classes of the English people. It was said they came to eat the bread of Englishmen and reduce the scale of wages; the latter, it was alleged, had already fallen from 18 pence to 15 pence where they were encamped. "It was also charged that they retained their love of their native land, corresponded with their friends in Germany and might act as spies, and eventually might even destroy the true British character of the race." These representations excited a rancorous prejudice against these unfortunates. To many Englishmen the name of German was synonymous with that of Roman Catholic. Hence the dislike and distrust with which the majority of the lower ranks among the English regarded these people. The Tories refused to employ or relieve any except such as were Protestants, and willing to become members of the Church of England. The French refugees who had settled there and who had themselves fled from persecution, are said to have been the most pitiless and jealous of all.[22]

---

[31] The "Theatrum Europaeum."

[22] Cassell's England. Geschichte und Zustanden, p. 43. Geschichsblätter, p. 24.

To many Englishmen, especially among the lower orders, the name of German was synonymous with that of Roman Catholic, and this fact served to intensify the dislike with which these colonists were regarded upon their arrival in England. It is hardly to be wondered at, therefore, if the lower classes of Englishmen not only did all they could to drive these Germans out of London, but should resort to actual violence to do so. According to Löher and Kapp, upon one occasion no fewer than 2000 infuriated Englishmen, armed with axes, scythes and smith hammers, made an attack upon one of the German encampments, and struck down all who did not flee. The same writers tell us that at this time there happened to be in London five chiefs of the Mohawk tribe of Indians, who had come to ask the assistance of her Majesty's Government against the attacks of the French in Canada. These, in the course of their wanderings in the neighborhood of London, came upon the Palatine encampment at Blackheath, and seeing their poverty and wretched condition, inquired as to the cause. Being told that the earnest longing of these people was lands in America where they could live and help themselves, they were so moved by what they heard, that they invited the Germans to come to them in America and offered Queen Anne a gift of rich lands whereon they might settle.[33]

---

[33] Löher: Die Deutchen in Amerika, p. 43. See also Hallische Nachrichten, 973-981.

But it was not those in the humbler walks of life alone who spoke unkindly of these miserable wanderers. Dean Swift had this untruthful fling at them: "Some persons, whom the voice of the nation authorizes me to call her enemies, taking advantage of the general naturalization act, had invited over a great number of foreigners of all religions, under the name of Palatines, who understood no trade or handicraft, yet rather chose to beg than labor; who, besides infesting our streets, bred contagious diseases by which we lost in natives thrice the number of population gained in foreigners."[84] In reply to this charge of the witty, but bitter, dean of St. Patrick's, I may say I have nowhere discovered any evidence of the charges he makes concerning an unusual mortality among the English people, through contact with the Palatines. If there was any cause whatever, it was doubtless exaggerated to lend point to the pen of a caustic Tory writer. It is not to be denied, however, that insufficient nourishment and exposure had introduced much sickness among them. The report to the House of Commons on April 14, 1711, of the Committee appointed to consider the petition of the Ministers, Church Wardens and Inhabitants of St. Olathe, in Southwark, County of Surrey, proves that. Swift's charge that they understood no trade or handicraft is wholly untrue, as the numerous lists made of these people show.[34a] That they did beg is true, but it was from necessity and not from choice,

---

[84] Examiner, 41, 45.

as a score of authorities fully prove, and none but him deny.

But it must not be supposed that the entire body of the English people were arrayed against these long-suffering wanderers. If they had plenty of enemies they also had some good friends. The great Duke of Marlborough spoke warmly in their favor before the Ministry, during the period of their greatest coming. They were of the race which had filled the ranks of that sturdy champion of Protestantism, Gustavus Adolphus, and Marlborough had himself seen their heroism displayed upon many a stricken field, under his own command. England needed soldiers, and he well knew the world had none better.

But no man did the Palatines better service than

---

[34] "At several Times, from the first of May last past, to the 18th of July 1709, there have been landed in England of these distressed Palatines, the exact Number of 10,000 Souls. Those that arrived at the two first Times, viz: from the first of May, to the 12th of June, consisted of Men having families, 1278; Wives, 1234; Widows, 89; unmarry'd Men, 384; unmarry'd Women, 106: Boys above 14 Years of Age, 379; Girls above 14 Years, 374; Boys under 14 Years, 1367; Girls under 14 Years, 1309. So that the whole Number of the two first Numbers landed, were 6,520.

Of these, there are Husbandmen and vine dressers, 1083; Schoolmasters, 10; Herdsmen, 4; Wheelwrights, 13; Smiths, 46; Cloth and Linnen Weavers, 66; Carpenters, 90; Bakers, 32; Masons, 48; Coopers and Brewers, 48; Joiners, 20; Shoemakers, 40; Taylors, 58; Butchers, 15; Millers, 27; Sadlers, 7; Stocking-weavers, 5; Tanners, 7; Miners, 3; Brick-makers, 6; Hatters, 3; Hunters, 5; Turners, 6; Surgeons, 3; Locksmiths, 2; Bricklayers, 4; Glasiers, 2; Hatters, 3; Silver-smiths, 2; Carvers, 2; 1 Cook and 1 Student. To which above 1500 being added, that arriv'd in the River of Thames, July 18, and others at other Times, whose Families, Trades and Employment are not yet distinguish'd or number'd, makes the Number of the Palatines amount in the whole to about 10,000 Souls." Palatine Refugees in England, pp. 19-20.

Bishop Burnet.[35] Early and late he was their steadfast champion. When the bill to naturalize such as were willing to take the oath of allegiance, and receive the sacrament in any Protestant Church, came

---

[35] Among the few men of prominence and influence, who during those trying times resolutely stood up and unselfishly endeavored to meliorate the condition of these Palatines, the name of Gilbert Burnet, Bishop of Salisbury, must ever occupy a foremost place. Next to the Queen herself, they seem to have had no better friend.

Burnet was born in Edinburg in 1643. He entered Marischal College, Aberdeen, at the age of ten. After taking his degree he gave himself to the study of law, and afterwards to Divinity. He studied Hebrew in Holland and later became Professor of Divinity in the University of Glasgow. He resigned his chair and went to London, where he was made chaplain to the Rolls Chapel and lecturer at St. Clements. In 1679-81 he published the first two volumes of his History of the Reformation, for which Parliament gave him a vote of thanks. He had sided with the moderate party and upon his refusal to attach himself to that of the King, he was deprived of his lectureship. After this he passed to the continent, travelling in Switzerland, Italy, France and Germany. He made the acquaintance of the Prince of Orange, with whom he became a favorite. When William came over to England, Burnet accompanied him as chaplain and in 1689 was made Bishop of Salisbury. He was of a disputatious temperament and was involved in many troubles in consequence. He was a voluminous author. He died in 1715 and his "History of his Own Time" was not published until after his death. In politics he was a Whig and in consequence was assailed by Swift, Pope and other Tory writers. He was a broad churchman, sincere in his views, of strict morality, great charity and moderation, honest and earnest, but sometimes inclined to be warped in his judgments.

Macaulay devotes several pages of his brilliant history to an analysis of Burnet's character. He alludes to his many faults of understanding and temper, but says: "Yet Burnet, though open in many respects to ridicule, and even to serious censure, was no contemptible man. His parts were quick, his industry unwearied, his reading various and most extensive. He was at once a historian, an antiquary, a theologian, a pamphleteer, a debater and an active political leader; and in every one of these he made himself conspicuous among able competitors." The value of the services of this man to the cause of the poor Palatines, which he so warmly espoused, can hardly be over-estimated.

Kneller Pinx.

GILBERT BURNET

BISHOP OF SALISBURY

OB. 1714-15.

up for action in the House of Lords, many of the ecclesiastical peers demanded that they should take it only in the Established Church, but Bishop Burnet, greatly to the scandal of his brethren, advocated any Protestant form, and carried the day.[36] The Bishop of Chester, a High Churchman, most earnestly opposed such liberal dealing with these foreign Protestants.

ADDRESS OF THE PALATINES.

The Palatines themselves, or some one in their behalf, issued the following address to the English people:

"We, the Poor Distressed *Palatines*, whose utter Ruin was occasioned by the Merciless Cruelty of a Bloody Enemy, the French, whose prevailing Power some Years past, like a torrent, rushed into our Country and overwhelmed us at once; and being not Content with Money and Food Necessary for their Occasions, not only dispossessed us of all Support but inhumanly burnt our Houses to the Ground, whereby being deprived of all Shelter, we were turned into the open Fields, there with our Families to seek what shelter we could find, were obliged to make the earth our Repository for Rest, and the clouds our Canopy or Covering.

"We poor wretches in this deplorable condition made our Humble Supplication and Cries to Almighty God, whose Omnisciency is extensive, who has promised to relieve all those that make their

---

[36] Cassell's History of England.

Humble Supplications to him that he will hear them ; Relieve them and Support them in what Condition soever; and likewise has promised to all those who shall feed the Hungry, Cloath the Naked, and Comfort the Distressed, they shall be received into his Everlasting Kingdom, where they shall be rewarded with Eternal Life.

"We magnify the Goodness of our Great God, who heard our Prayers, and in his good Time disposed the Hearts of Good and Pious Princes to a Christian Compassion and Charity towards us in this deplorable State, by whose Royal Bounties, and the large Donations of well disposed Quality and Gentry, we and our Children have been preserved from perishing with Hunger; but especially since our Arrival in this Land of Canaan, abounding with all Things necessary and convenient for Humane Life.

"Blessed Land! Governed by the Mother of *Europe*, and the Best of Queens, in her Steadfastness and great Alacrity in Contributing largely, in all Respects, towards all her allies abroad for the speedy Reducing of the Exhorbitant Power of *France*, and our great Enemy, and likewise her Great Piety and Mild Government, and great Charity towards all Her Distressed Subjects at Home: And not Bounded here, but from afar has gathered Strangers and Despicable creatures (as a Hen her Chickens under her Wings) Scattered abroad, Destitute, Hungry, Naked, and in want of every Thing necessary for our Support.

"This great Act of Charity towards us obliges us

and our Posterity to perpetuate Her name in our Families, and to render our Hearty Prayers to Almighty God, that he will be pleased to Bless Her Sacred Majesty with Long Life, and a Prosperous Reign, and this Nation with a Happy Peace and Plenty; and for the better obtaining of which may be given Her Repeated Victories over Her Enemies, which are the Redundant Rewards and Blessings of God upon Her in this Life, and may She be blest with an Immortal Crown that never fades.

"We humbly intreat all Tradesmen not to Repine at the good Disposition of Her Sacred Majesty, and of the Quality and Gentry; but with great Compassion join with them in their Charitable Disposition towards us, and with a cheerful Readiness Receive us at this Juncture, which we hope will be a means to redouble the Blessings of God upon this Nation.

"We Intreat you to lay aside all Reflections and Imprecations, and Ill Language against us, for that is contradictory to a Christian Spirit, and we do assure you it shall be our Endeavours to act with great Humility and Gratitude, and to render our Prayers for you, which is all the Returns that can be made by your[98a]

DISTRESSED BRETHREN,
The Palatines.

The English people manifested much interest in the religious well being of these sojourners. This arose from diverse reasons, however. It was feared

---

[98a] State of the Palatines, p. 6.

Umständige Geographische Beschreibung

Der zu allerletzt erfundenen

Provintz

PENSYLVA-NIÆ,

In denen End-Gräntzen

AMERICÆ

In der West-Welt gelegen,

Durch

FRANCISCUM DANIELEM PASTORIUM,

J. V. Lic. und Friedens-Richtern daselbsten.

Worbey angehencket sind einige notable Begebenheiten/ und Bericht-Schreiben an dessen Herrn Vattern

MELCHIOREM ADAMUM PASTORIUM,

Und andere gute Freunde.

Franckfurt und Leipzig/
Zufinden bey Andreas Otto. 1704.

by some that if they remained permanently, they might join the ranks of the Dissenters; others interested themselves in their behalf because they wished to swell the ranks of the Established Church. A pamphlet was prepared in German and English for the use of the Palatines. It contained an address admonishing them to obey their Lord and Master's commands and follow in the footsteps of his disciples, and to shun the works of the devil. It also included the Sermon on the Mount and several chapters of the gospel of St. Matthew. Several pages were composed especially for their benefit; first a general thanksgiving, a prayer for the Queen, one for times of great tribulation and one for morning and night, and for God's grace and blessing.

Some of the Catholics who were of Protestant descent changed their religion with alacrity. Those who were Lutherans communed in both the German and English churches. The proprietors of the Carolinas having manifested a disposition to take married men only to their colonies, this led to numerous marriages among such as came over unmarried.

But all the while that these temporary arrangements for the care of these people were going on, the Government was not unmindful of the fact that sooner or later some permanent disposition of them must be made. In all, nearly 14,000 had come and with the exception of a few who had secured employment and were self sustaining, they were supported at the public charge. A contract was made with a merchant in the West Indies to send five hundred families to Barbadoes. I have not been able to find any evidence that this contract was carried out. Most probably it was not.

A plan to locate a large number in Ireland was brought forward and consummated, but I have deemed this Irish colony, in view of its numbers and character, deserving of a special chapter which will follow.

The plan to locate them throughout the different counties of the kingdom was not given up. Lord Sunderland, who was the Secretary of State, wrote, among other letters, one to the Mayor of Canterbury, asking him to receive and permanently locate some of them. The letter was referred to the town Magistrates, who declined to take them upon the ground that their own poor were a heavy burden.

But the bounty of £5 per head which, as has already been mentioned, was offered to all parishes who would accept and settle Palatines, met with acceptance in some localities. Under its provisions, Germans in limited numbers found their way into all parts of England. As the bounty, rather than the welfare of the immigrant was the main object in view by the communities that accepted these conditions, little attention was given to them thereafter, and they were left to take care of themselves in the best way they could. The result was that many became dissatisfied with their lot after a while. They found no companionship among the English, who, as a rule, disliked as well as despised them, and, longing for the association of their countrymen, many of them again found their way back to London and the various camps in the vicinity. There were some, however, who, located at great distances from the great metropolis, were from that cause, poverty and other reasons compelled to remain where they had been sent. From the large number that remains unaccounted for, after summing up those who were sent out of the country, the conclusion seems irresistible that some thousands remained for a term of years, or permanently, scattered throughout the United Kingdoms, and the city of London no doubt retained her full share.

Captain Elkin of the English navy came forward with the proposition that 600 of them should be settled on the Scilly Islands, a small group off the southwest coast of England. Lord Sunderland thought well of the project, and on September 21, and October 2, 1709, two transports were sent down the Thames with 600 men on board, well provisioned and otherwise well provided for. For some unexplained reason, these men were never sent to their destination, but after remaining on ship board three entire months, they were again set on shore on December 30, of the same year, and found their way back to Blackheath. The cost of this miserable failure was £821.18.5 for ship hire, and £665.0.6½ more for victualling the same; a total of £1486.18.-11½.

Such of them as were Catholics, and refused to become Protestants, were returned to Holland at

Queen Anne's cost, and furnished with the needed supplies to reach their own countries.

Seeing no prospects of a speedy release from their wretched condition, one hundred and fifty of the able-bodied young men enlisted in the army and were sent to serve in Lord Gallaway's regiment then on duty in Portugal. According to Luttrell's diary some also enlisted in Lord Haye's regiment. Some enlisted as sailors in the navy and were sent into foreign parts.[57] Death, too, came along and committed havoc in their ranks. More than a thousand died in the encampment at Blackheath, happy in their release from want and misery. They were reluctant to be scattered all over the British dominions. Their hope had been to be settled together in the colonies of the New World, and to this desire they remained constant throughout all their terrible experiences.

In April, 1709, the proprietors of Carolina had sold to two persons, Lewis Michell and Christopher De Graffenreid, ten thousand acres of land, in one body between the Neuse and Cape Fear rivers. Michell had previously been in the employ of the Canton of Bern, Switzerland, to look for lands in Pennsylvania, Virginia or the Carolinas, whereon a Swiss colony might be settled by that Canton, but the latter having given up the project, Michell and his partner conceived the idea of bringing over colo-

---

[57] "Etliche Sind mit der Ost Indischen Flatte in Ost Indien gangen, und daselbs zerstrenet." Das verlangte, nicht erlangte Canaan, p. 8.

Some Sent to the Carolinas. 317

Außführlich und Umständlicher Bericht
Von der berühmten Landschafft
CAROLINA,
In dem Engelländischen America gelegen.

An Tag gegeben Von

Kocherthalern.

Zweyter Druck.

Franckfurt am Mäyn/
Zu finden bey Georg Heinrich Oehrling/
Anno 1709.

PAMPHLET CIRCULATED BY KOCHERTHAL, ADVISING EMIGRANTS
TO GO TO THE CAROLINAS.

nists themselves.[38] The Palatines became the object of their speculative enterprise, and they covenanted with the English Commissioners, that the latter should send over about one hundred families, in all about 650 persons, and locate them on these lands. The Commissioners allowed five pounds per head for the transporting of these settlers, supplied them with provisions for twelve months, and in addition gave them twenty shillings each out of the funds which had been raised by popular subscription. The colonists reached the confluence of the Neuse and Trent rivers in December, 1709, and were housed in temporary shelters. In accordance with instructions from the home government, Governor Tryon allotted 100 acres to each man, woman and child.

A large number, perhaps as many as two or three thousand, were returned to the places from which they had originally come. Luttrell mentions that in May, 1710, Minister Dayrolle gave five florins each to 800 Palatines who were returned to their homes. Some of these, as we have already seen, were Catholics, but many Protestants were also sent along, it being found impossible to dispose of them otherwise.

The last large body to be sent away was the well-known colony that went to the State of New York under the plan submitted by Col. Hunter, then recently appointed Governor of that province, to the Board of Trade. It is not necessary that I should go into the details of this scheme, as they are

---

[38] Williamson's North Carolina.

The New York Colony. 319

familiar to all, and will be fully dealt with in a future paper of this series. It is enough to say that three thousand two hundred were crowded into ten small ships and set sail in March, 1710. They arrived at intervals between June 14 and July 24. Four hundred and seventy perished on the voyage.

Not all, however, left England. Some had found permanent employment and a few had entered into business. Some worked in her Majesty's gardens and others on a canal at Windsor. A little hamlet arose on the west side of London where some houses had been erected for the use of these people, and to this day they bear the name of the Palatine houses.[39]

An account written at the period, gives us an insight into their manner of living at that time:

THIS QUAINT WOOD CUT OF THE PERIOD SHOWS HOW THESE PEOPLE PASSED THEIR TIME WHILE CAMPED AT BLACKHEATH.

"They spend their time very religiously and industriously, having prayers morning and evening,

---

[39] H. A. Holmes.

with singing of psalms, and preaching every Sunday, where both old and young appear very serious and devout. Some employ themselves in making several toys of small value, which they sell to the multitudes that come daily to see them. They are contented with very ordinary food, their bread being brown, and their meat of the coarsest and cheapest sort, which, with a few roots and herbs, they eat with much cheerfulness and thankfulness. Great numbers of them go every Sunday to their church in the Savoy and receive the Sacrament of their own ministers. Many of the younger are married every week; the women wear rosemary and the men laurel in their hair at the time of their marriage, adultery and fornication being much abhorred by them. When any are buried, all the attendants go singing after the corpse, and when they come to the grave the coffin is opened for all to see the body. After it is

PALATINES WORSHIPPING IN ST. MARY'S, OF SAVOY.

laid in the ground they all sigh again for some time and then depart. They carry grown people upon a bier and children upon their heads. On the whole they appear to be an innocent, laborious, peaceable, healthy and ingenious people, and may be rather reckoned a blessing than a burden to any nation where they shall be settled."

To give some idea of the class of persons who composed this great body of immigrants, the following list is submitted. I have found a number of such lists,[40] but the one I quote is the fullest of them all and no doubt as reliable as any. This authority says that " from the middle of April, 1709, till the middle of July, the arrivals in London were 11,294 German Protestants, males and females. Of the males there were : husbandmen and vine dressers, 1838; bakers, 78; masons, 477; carpenters, 124; shoemakers, 68; tailors, 99: butchers, 29; millers, 45; tanners, 14; stocking weavers, 7; saddlers, 13; glass blowers, 2; hatters, 3; lime burners, 8; schoolmasters, 18; engravers, 2; brickmakers, 3; silversmiths, 2; smiths, 35; herdsmen, 3; blacksmiths, 48; potters, 3; turners, 6; barbers, 1; surgeons, 2. Of these 11,294 there were 2556 who had families."[41]

---

[40] State of the Palatines.

Rupp's note in Rush's Essay on the manners and customs of the Germans of Pennsylvania

[41] As a matter of interest a second enumeration is given from Frank's "*Frankfurter Mesz-Kalender von Ostern bis Herbst,*" 1709, which says that by the middle of July 6520 Germans had arrived in London. Of these 1278 were men with families. 1238 married women, 89 widows, 384 young men, 106 young women, 379 boys over 14 years old. 374 girls over 14 years old, 1363 boys under 14 and 1309 girls under 14 years.

Among these people were 1083 husbandmen and vine dressers, 90

Kurtze Beschreibung
Deß H. R. Reichs Stadt
Windsheim/

Samt

Dero vielfältigen Unglücks-Fällen/ und wahrhafftigen Ursachen ihrer so grossen Decadenz und Erbarmungs-würdigen Zustandes/

Aus

Alten glaubwürdigen Documentis und Briefflichen Urkunden (der itzo lebenden lieben Burgerschafft/ und Dero Nachkommen/ zu guter Nachricht) also zusammen getragen/ und in den Druck gegeben

durch

Melchiorem Adamum Pastorium, ältern Burgemeistern und Ober-Richtern in besagter Stadt.

Gedruckt zu Nürnberg
bey Christian Sigmund Froberg.
Im Jahr Christi 1692.

Fortunately for us, who are at this distant day attempting to unravel the twisted threads which encumber the story of these poor Palatines, there lived in London at that time a man of education, leisure, and thoroughly acquainted with public affairs. His name was Narcissus Luttrell. One of his pleasures was to keep a diary. This diary is very full and minute, but unlike the better known diarist who preceded him, the inimitable Pepys, he devoted his pages more to public affairs and less to himself. From day to day, for a period of 36 years, he recorded the World's news as it reached London. Every thing was set down as it came. He appears to have been without bias or prejudices and as the result, his diary appears to be a complete picture of the times as they passed before him. It contains numerous allusions to this Palatine immigration, and as it is little known, I will here quote such remarks as I have found in it bearing on this question.

"1709 Thursday, May 12. From Cologne that three great vessels more were arrived there with Protestants from the Palatines for England, and thence to Pennsylvania; so that above 1000 families have already quitted that country.

"Saturday, 14 May. A great many poor German and French Protestants have taken the oaths this

---

carpenters, 34 bakers, 48 masons, 20 joiners, 40 shoemakers, 58 tailors, 15 butchers, 27 millers, 7 tanners, 4 stocking weavers, 6 barbers, 3 locksmiths, 13 smiths, 46 linen and cloth weavers, 48 coopers, 13 wheelwrights, 5 hunters, 7 saddlers, 2 glass blowers, 2 hatters, 8 lime and tile burners, 1 cook, 10 schoolmasters, 1 student, 2 engravers, 7 farmers.

week at the Queen's bench court, in order to their naturalization by the late act.

"Saturday, 28 May. Sunday last about 300 Protestants from the Palatinate received the sacrament at the Prussian church in Savoy, in order to their naturalization; 1300 more are also arrived, and a sermon will be preached before them once a week in Aldgate church.

"Tuesday, 14 June. Sunday Monsieur du Quesne, a French Protestant, presented a letter to her majestie from the King of Prussia about the Reformed churches in France, and a petition in the name of above a million of those poor people who groan under a most severe persecution; she assured him she had already given her ministers abroad instructions concerning the same, and will doe for them what else lies in her power.

"Thursday, 16 June. The justices of the Middlesex have resolved to petition her majestie for a brief to support the poor Palatines come over hither, being upward of 6000.

"Saturday, 18 June. Tis said a brief was then ordered (in council) for a collection in London and Middlesex to relieve the poor Palatines, and that the Commissioners of Trade and Plantations are to take care of them till the West India fleet goes, when they are to embark for Nevis and St. Christophers, to repeople those islands destroyed by the French.

"Tuesday, 21 June. Tents are putting up at Blackheath for the poor Palatines till they can be transported to the West Indies.

"Thursday, 7 July. Yesterday the nobility and gentry, commissioners for providing for the support of the poor Palatines lately arrived here, met the first time in the convocation house at St. Paul's, where were present the Lord Mayor and several of the aldermen.

"Tuesday, 12 July. Monsieur Ruperti is translating the liturgy of the church of England into High Dutch, which books are to be given among the poor Palatines, 2000 more of whom last Sunday arrived here from Rotterdam.

"Saturday, 16 July. The lords proprietors of Carolina have made proposals to a committee of Council, to take all the Palatines here, from 15 to 45 years old and send them to their plantation; but her majestie to be at the charge of transporting them, which will be above £10 a head.

"Saturday, 23 July. 300 more Palatines are arrived, so that the whole number here is about 8000.

"Saturday, 1 August. Several of the poor Palatines who came lately over, and were Papists, have renounced that religion, and more of them, 'tis expected, will do the like.

"Thursday, 4 August. Mr. Paul Girard at an eminent French refugee merchant in Coleman street, has upon the brief for the poor Palatines, given £423 towards their relief, and several other citizens very liberally.

"Tuesday, 9 August. The Commissioners for providing for the poor Palatines, upon inspecting the subscriptions of the nobility and gentry, find that

CONTINUATIO
Der
Beschreibung der Landschafft
PENSYLVANIÆ
An denen End-Gräntzen
AMERICÆ.
Uber vorige des Herrn Pastorii
Relationes.

In sich haltend:
Die Situation, und Fruchtbarkeit des Erdbodens. Die Schiffreiche und andere Flüsse. Die Anzahl derer bißhero gebauten Städte. Die seltsame Creaturen an Thieren/ Vögeln und Fischen. Die Mineralien und Edelgesteine. Deren eingebohrnen wilden Völcker Sprachen/ Religion und Gebräuche. Und die ersten Christlichen Pflantzer und Anbauer dieses Landes.

Beschrieben von
GABRIEL THOMAS
15. Jährigen Inwohner dieses Landes.

Welchem Tractätlein noch beygefüget sind:
Des Hn. DANIEL FALCKNERS Burgers und Pilgrims in Pensylvania 193. Beantwortungen uff vorgelegte Fragen von guten Freunden.

Franckfurt und Leipzig/
Zu finden bey Andreas Otto/ Buchhändlern.

about £15,000 is already given for their support. Abundance of them are gone hence in wagons for Chester to embark for Ireland, and the rest designed for that Kingdom will speedily follow.

"Thursday, 15 September. The Popish Palatines who came hither, are ordered to go home, having passports for the same.

"Thursday, 29 September. Yesterday 18 Palatines listed themselves in the Lord Haye's regiment.

"Thursday, 6 Oct. The commissioners for settling the poor Palatines have resolved to send forthwith 600 of them to Carolina, and 1500 of them to New York; and 'tis said, the merchants of Bediford and Barnstable, concerned in the Newfoundland fishery, intend to employ 500 more in their service.

"Thursday, 29 Dec. Colonel Hunter (the new Governor of New York,) designs next week to embark for his government of New York; and most of the Palatines remaining here goe with him to people that colony.

"1710. Thursday, 25 May. Mr. Ayrolles, the British Secretary at the Hague, is gone for Rotterdam to distribute her majesties charity to 800 poor Palatines returning home, being 5 florins to each person.

"Thursday, 27 July. The first ticket of the State lottery drawn yesterday entitled the fortunate holder to £50 per annum, and fell upon Mr. Walter Cocks of Camberwell, who so generously supported the Palatines last year, and has this year the best crop of corn for quantity in all the county of Surrey."

THE GERMAN COLONY IN IRELAND.[42]

ITS FOUNDING AND ITS VICISSITUDES—IT INTRODUCED THE LINEN INDUSTRY INTO THAT COUNTRY—WHAT TRAVELLERS HAVE HAD TO SAY OF ITS PEOPLE AND THEIR CONDITION.

SEAL OF THE CITY OF LIMERICK.

I RETURN now to those Germans who were not sent to America, who were not returned to their own country, and who did not remain in England, the 3800 souls that were colonized in Ireland. Beyond the few brief allusions to their transportation to that country found in modern writers, comparatively little concerning them is known to the general reader. I shall, therefore, proceed to give with some detail, the information that has rewarded my research concerning them.

As we have already seen, the attempt to settle these people permanently in England met with no favor and had to be abandoned. The plan to send some to Ireland and locate them permanently there, apparently met with no opposition. In fact, the proposition to make this disposal of them originated in Ireland itself. The Committee appointed to inquire into the coming of the Palatines into Great Britain, and upon what encouragement, in their report to the House of Commons on April 14, 1711, said that the plan for locating some of them in Ireland, originated in that country itself. Mr. J. Marshall, Deputy Master of the Rolls of Tipperary, offered to assume the care of 1000, and build houses for them. At the request of the Lord Lieutenant and Council of Ireland, he addressed the Queen on the subject, asking that as many Palatines should be sent there as her Majesty should think proper. In

---

[43] The following order was issued from White Hall, July 27, 1709: "The Right Honorable the Lord Lieutenant and Council of Ireland, having in an Humble Address to her Majesty, Requested, that as many of the poor Palatines as her Majesty shall see fit, may be settled in that Kingdom, and given Assurances that they shall be very Kindly received, and advantageously settled there; and the address having been laid before the Right Honorable, the Lords and others, her Majesty's Commissioners, for receiving and disposing of the money to be collected for the subsistence and settlement of the said Palatines The said Commissioners have resolved that Five Hundred Families of the said Palatines be forthwith sent into that Kingdom, and refer it to their Committee to settle the manner and time of sending them thither."

August, 1709, 500 families, numbering in all 3000 persons, were sent to that country. The cost of sending them there as disclosed in the Parliamentary report, was £3498.16.6. To complete their settlement in Ireland a warrant was drawn and signed by Queen Anne, for the sum of £15,000, to be paid out of her Majesty's revenues in that country, and to be repaid in three years, at the rate of £5000 every year.

The report to the Commons informs us that in Feb. 1710, 800 more Palatines were sent from London by way of Chester or Liverpool, to Ireland, upon representations from the Lord Lieutenant, the crown again bearing the charges, and £9000 were allotted for their better settlement, this sum, like the former one, being also made a charge on the Irish revenues. Presently, however, it was found that some of these families were returning to England again, and that still others were preparing to follow them. Whereupon the Commissioners sent an agent, one John Crockett, to prevent, if possible, any further migrations. Upon arriving in Ireland, he found 20 families ready to go on board a vessel to return to England, they having a pass for 25 families. This pass was signed by the Lord Lieutenant's Steward, John Smalles. Crockett however stopped them and took away their pass. An appeal was taken to the highest legal tribunal and he was informed by Lord Chief Justice Broderick, that being a free people, they could not be legally prevented from going where they would. That decision seems to have effectually disposed of Agent Crockett and his mission. Within

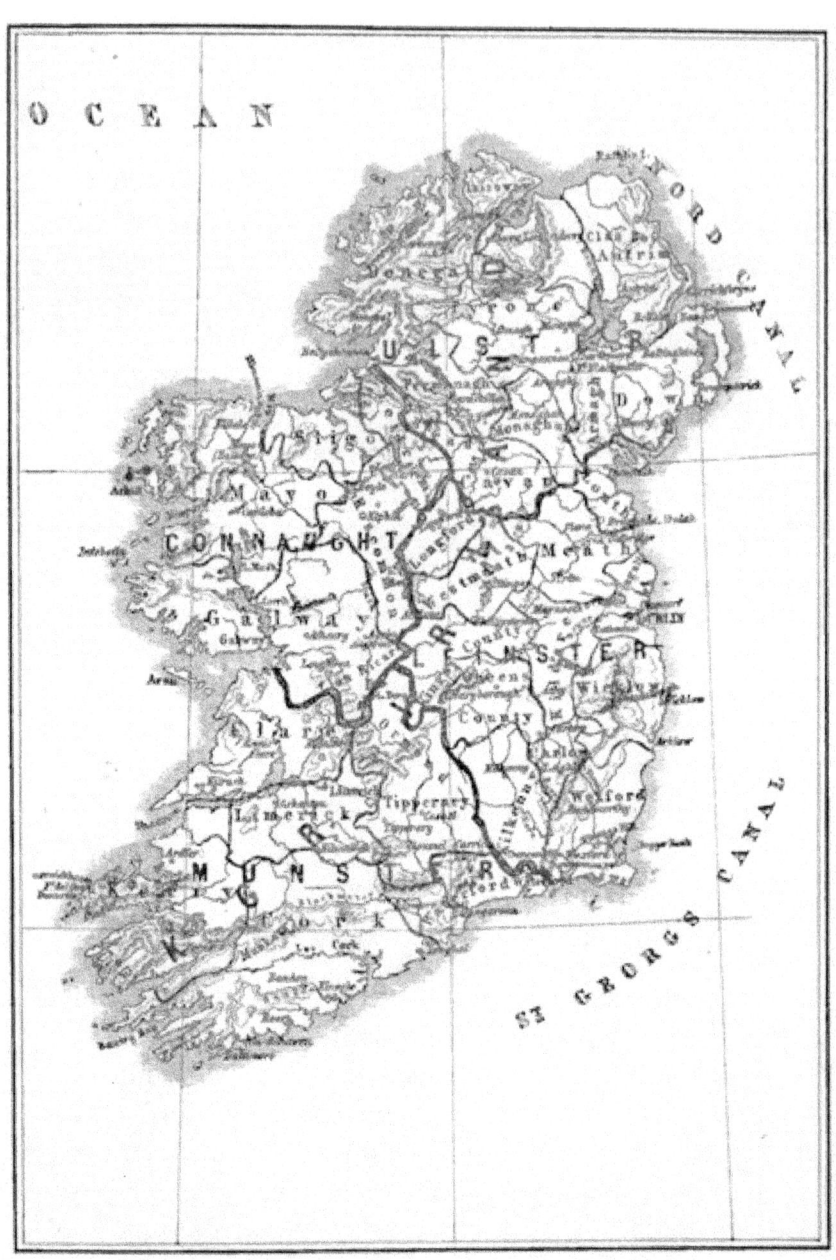

Map of Ireland at the time of the German Exodus.

a brief period thereafter, 232 more families returned to Southwark.

The reasons these Palatines gave for leaving Ireland, was the rough usage received from the Commissary in whose charge they were, a man named Huick, from a Mr. Street, and others, who did not pay them their subsistance, they having received but one week's allowance. They paid their own passage to England, although they were told they should have ten shillings per head for leaving Ireland. From all this we think we have ample reasons to infer that this German colony partook somewhat of the nature of a speculation in which the public officials took a leading part. Why was the Lord Lieutenant of Ireland so anxious to get them into that country, and why was he so busily employed in sending them away again, after the large allowances for their maintenance had been received? Even the pittance of ten shillings, which appears to have been the bribe offered them to go back again, it seems was not paid. Apparently, there was an undercurrent of fraud throughout on the part of the minor and higher officials.

The motives for sending these Palatines to Ireland was by no means an unselfish one, even on the part of the Government itself, or intended only to better their condition. Being Protestants the House of Commons was of the opinion that so large a body of that creed would not only tranquilize, but contribute to the stability and security of the Kingdom which has not yet recovered from the shock of the battle of

the Boyne, fought only twenty years before. To a
certain extent this last aim was defeated because their
treatment and deception by the government agents
drove some of them away before they were quietly
settled down.

They were located on some unimproved lands at Rathkeale, near Limerick, in the County of Munster. Kapp says that among the first 500 families sent to Ireland were all the linen weavers, and this is also spoken of by other writers.[43] Whether the linen industry was prominent in Ireland prior to this invasion of the Palatines I have not been able to ascertain, but it is a matter of history that in the year 1711, two years after this colony was founded, a government board of manufacturers was established in Ireland, which, by means of a system of bounties and in other ways did its utmost to encourage the linen trade."[44] These facts

ARMS OF THE BISHOP OF LIMERICK.

---

[43] Friedrich Kapp. Geschichtsblätter, p. 23.

[44] Anton Eickhoff: In der neuen Heimath; Geschichtliche Mittheilungen uber die deutchen einwanderer in aller Theilen der Uuion, has copied Kapp verbatim. Kapp's words are: "Zuerst 500 Familien, darunter alle Leinweber, etc."

seem to warrant the belief, that if these German colonists did not in fact, first establish the linen trade in that country, they at all events gave it such an impulse with their skill as to have for nearly two hundred years made it the most important textile industry in Ireland.[45] Such it is to-day.

In 1715, Parliament passed a special act authorizing the naturalization of those who were still there, 213 families in all. Of those who went away, about 75 families returned to London, from whence they were sent to this country. For a number of years afterward, numbers of them kept coming to Pennsylvania. The expense of sending them to Ireland and their settlement there, cost the English government £24,000.

From the fact that for a good many years little was heard of this colony, we may infer that German thrift and industry were making their mark there, as they have done the whole world over; that they pursued the even tenor of their way, and gave little care to what was going on around them.

Under the distinctive "name of Palatines, they left the impress of their character in social and economical traits on the whole district, extending from Castle Mattrass eastward to Adare."[46]

John Wesley, the eminent evangelist, and founder of Methodism, during a trip to Ireland, in 1758, paid a visit to this Palatine colony. In his Journal he

---

[45] Chamber's Encyclopaedia, vol. vi.
[46] Holmes.

Teusday evening

The enclosed petitions weare given mee as I came from S:t James's, one I beleive is from y:e man you gave me an account of yesterday, y:e other haveing a wife & six children makes one think it a case of Compassion, however I desire you would informe your self about it as soon as you can possible, & if you find it soe, take care his life may be saved, I am

      Your very affectionate
      freind
          ANNE R.

It affords me much pleasure to be able to present the above brief but most interesting autograph letter of Queen Anne. There is no address and no evidence to show to whom it was written. The familiar tone seems to indicate that the person was one of her political household. Possibly it may have been to one of the clergymen who played so prominent a part in this drama of exile although this is not likely. Be this as tells what he saw while there. He says: "I rode over to Court Mattrass, a colony of Germans, whose parents came out of the Palatinate fifty years ago. Twenty families settled here; twenty more at Killikeen, a mile off; fifty at Balligarene, about two miles eastward, and twenty at Pallas, four miles further. Each family had a few acres of ground, on which they built as many little houses. They are since considerably increased in number of families. Having no minister, they were becoming eminent for drunkenness, cursing, swearing, and an utter neglect of religion. But they are washed since they heard the truth which is able to save their souls. An oath is now rarely heard among them, or a drunkard seen in their borders. Court Mattrass is built in the form of a square, in the middle of which they have placed a pretty large preaching house."[47] In 1760, some of the descendants of these Irish Palatines left Limerick for the United States, and were among the pioneers of American Methodism. John Wesley had made a good many converts among these people while he was with them, the principal having been Philip Embury, (Amberg) and his son Samuel, the latter having come to New York in 1760.[48]

---

it may, however, we have in this most kind and womanly note, confirming evidence of the unselfish interest this noble Queen felt in these people.

The original of this letter is in the incomparable collection of Ferdinand J. Dreer, Esq., of Philadelphia. This fac-simile is here, by permission, for the first time, given to the public.

[47] See Wesley's Journal.

[48] Rupp's unpublished MSS. See Seidensticker's German Day, p. 17.

Eight acres of land, according to one account, were set aside for each one of these Germans at five shillings per acre, and the Government pledged itself to pay the ground taxes for them, for a period of twenty years.

An English "Blue Book" states that "they were a frugal and industrious people. Their number, however, has been greatly diminished through later emigrations to America, and at the present day (period unknown) there are proportionately but few descendants of these in Ireland."

In 1780, Farrar, the historian of Limerick, wrote of them as follows: "The Palatines still retain their language, but it is on the point of declining. They elect a Burgomaster, to whom they appeal in all cases of dispute. They are industrious and have leases from the landlords at reasonable rents. They are better fed and clothed than the Irish farmers. Their husbandry and harvests are better than those of their Irish neighbors. By degrees they abandoned their 'Saur Kraut' and lived on potatoes, milk, butter, oat and wheat bread, and poultry. They sleep between two beds (feather beds), huge flitches of bacon hang from the rafters, and massive chests hold the household linen: their superstitions savor of the banks of the Rhine: in their dealings they are upright and honorable."

In 1840, Mr. and Mrs. S. C. Hall, the well known authors, also visited and wrote about this old German colony. They said: "They differ from other people of the country. The elder people still retain their language, customs and religion, but the younger ones mingle with the Irish people and intermarry with them."

In May of the same year, Dr. Michell writes: "The majority of them have decidedly foreign features, and are of sturdy build. Their countenance is of a dark hue, their hair dark and their eyes brown. A comparison of the inhabitants of the Bavarian Palatinate shows them to be light of complexion and blue eyed. This argues that the Irish Palatines have intermarried with the Irish natives. The old comfortable homes of these people are falling into decay, and newer dwellings have arisen nearby, some of them two stories high, with slate roofs. Almost all of them have gardens, and some orchards attached. Economy and industry prevail among them. The names of the Palatines in Ireland differ but little from those of people with the same origin. Some of their names are Baker, Miller, Lodwig, Modlar, Pyfer, Reynard, Shire, and Stark, which were originally Becker, Müller, Ludwig. Pfeiffer, Reinhardt and Shier."[50]

An intelligent traveller who made a tour of Ireland in 1840, and wrote a book about the country, throws out a most interesting suggestion in what he has to say of these people. This is what he writes: "It was also with much regret that I forebore from visiting a German colony that settled in the county of Limerick about the beginning of the last century.

---

[50] See article in the Philadelphia Record, a year or two ago.

The settlers were from the Palatinate, and their descendants are still called Palatinates, though they have lost the language of their fathers. They have not, however, lost the German character for good order and honorable dealing, and are looked upon as the best farmers in the country. 'They are a most respectable people,' said an Irish lady to me, 'and much wealthier and far better off than any of their Irish neighbors.'

"It is a constant subject of discussion in Ireland, between the Irish patriots and the adherents of the English, that is between the Celtomanes and the Anglomanes, whether the misery and poverty of Ireland ought to be attributed to the tyranny and bad government of the English, or whether the indolence and want of energy of the Irish themselves be not in a great measure to blame. Now the prosperity of this German colony, though subject to the same laws and influences as the native Irish, would seem not to decide the question in favor of the friends of the Celts. Upon the whole, however, there are not many Germans in Ireland, not even in Dublin. They were probably never more numerous there than during the rebellion in 1798, when several regiments of Hanoverians were employed in the country, and their presence in such form may not have left a very favorable impression respecting them on the public mind."[51]

Several authorities confirm the fact that as late as

---

[51] Ireland. By J. G Kohl, 1844.

1855, the descendants of these German-Irish colonists were still living in the county of Limerick and that to some extent they still retained many of their original characteristics along with their industry and thrift, and were scrupulously honorable in all their dealings. They were still, for the most part, prosperous farmers and weavers, and stood well in the community.[52]

We are, therefore, warranted in believing that on the whole, this Irish colony is to be regarded as having emerged from its troubles and trials as well, if not better, than any of the unwelcome visitors that poured into London in the spring and summer of 1709. It is true, some were dissatisfied and left, as has already been shown. Those who remained escaped the pest ships, and the tyranny that awaited them in the State of New York and elsewhere. Their greatest trials had come to an end, and thence forward neither religious nor political troubles molested them, while want and starvation existed only as unhappy memories.

---

[52] Meth. Quar. Rev. Oct. 1855.
See also Fliegende Blætter 11.36.

CONCLUSION.

ESTIMATE OF THE NUMBER OF THE GERMAN IMMIGRANTS—WHERE THEY WERE SENT AND SOMETHING ABOUT THOSE WHO REMAINED.

ARMS OF WURTEMBERG.

IT will be seen from the foregoing, that the large number which is said to have come to London, is not fully accounted for in the enumeration of those who were sent to Ireland, to the New World or returned to their own country again. Kapp, a reliable guide in general, fixes the total number of emigrants at between 13,000 and 14,000 souls. But he fails to dispose of that number when he comes to sum up. Löher goes far beyond him and says ship load after ship load reached London, until their number in the Blackheath camp reached 32,468. It would be interesting to know where he got his extravagant figures. There is no warrant for them in any published documents that I have seen, nor in the unpublished archives of England and Holland so far as they have been examined.

In this statement he is, however, followed by several later writers, who bring forward no evidence nor authority for their estimates. They seem to have followed Löher blindly. The statement, therefore, made by the latest author who has dealt with this phase of the question, that "During the two years 1708 and 1709, over thirty thousand of them crossed over to England,"[38] is wholly unsustained by the authorities, figures and facts to which I have had access.

Careful accounts of all the expenditures incurred by the British Government are to be found in the Journals of Parliament, and the records of the Board of Trade, and the sum total has been figured out. They include the costs incurred by the several schemes which have here been enumerated and nothing more. Had the Palatines been 32,000 instead of 14,000 or less, the cost must also have been doubled. As here given, the following numbers are accounted for:

Sent to Ireland,	3,800
Colonized in North Carolina,	650
Sent to New York,	3,200
Returned to Germany, (perhaps)	2,000
Died in England,	1,500
Enlisted, (perhaps)	350
Total	11,500

This enumeration leaves about two thousand unaccounted for. It is very probable that not all were sent out of the country, because some had found acceptable employment, while many left at intervals during the next few years. That some remained in London years after the great body of them had been disposed of is absolutely proven by a writer under the date of June, 1712, who says: "On my return (from Kensington and Hyde Park), I saw a number of the Palatines, the most poor, ragged creatures that I ever saw, and great objects of charity, if real exiles for religion."[54]

---

[53] Sydney George Fisher: The Making of Pennsylvania.
[54] Ralph Thoresly Diary, 1674-1724. 2 vols. 8 vo. London, 1830.

ARMS OF HANOVER.

COST OF MAINTAINING THESE GERMANS.

IT MEANT MORE THAN HALF A MILLION DOLLARS TO THE ENGLISH GOVERNMENT—BUT IT WAS MONEY WELL SPENT.

ARMS OF FRANKFORT.

ALL Germans, and more especially we Americans of German descent, owe a heavy debt of gratitude to Great Britain, the Government as well as her individual citizens, for what they did for those forlorn and distressed Palatines. While there can be no manner of doubt that the Government covertly, if not openly, connived at this immigration, there is also every reason to believe that it finally assumed far greater proportions than were looked for in the beginning; and, therefore, proved far more costly than was at first anticipated.

From first to last, and during every stage of its

progress, this remarkable episode proved a very costly affair to the English government. The records are still accessible, and from them the following statement is prepared:

To Kocherthal and his followers, £346.00; for the maintenance of these people at Rotterdam, and their transportation to England, £6199.3.2; collected by public subscription in London, and throughout the country, £19,838.11.1; cost of the Scilly Islands fiasco, £1487.18.11½; sending the colony to Ireland and expenses incurred thereby, £24,000; the cost of sending the remaining large body to New York, £38,000; the Secretary of the Navy also expended £8,000 in various ways; there were besides many other charges for smaller amounts, which ran the figures up to a total of £135,775.18. There is some doubt whether the entire sum voted for the settlement of the Irish colony was paid out, or the total allotted for the care of those sent to New York, but this is not material. Here we have more than a half a million dollars paid out, at a period when England was not so rich as she is now, and at a time, too, when she was engaged in costly foreign wars, and when money was worth much more than it is to-day. While it is perhaps true that mercenary motives may have had much to do with her early action, it is also undoubtedly true that her Government was far-sighted enough to understand, that the accession of so many of the best citizens of one of the richest provinces in the Old World, must have its due effect upon the welfare and prosperity of the colonies she

Curieuse Nachricht Von PENSYLVANIA in Norden-America

Welche/
Auf Begehren guter Freunde/
Uber vorgelegte 103. Fragen/ bey seiner Abreiß aus Teutschland nach obigem Lande Anno 1700. ertheilet/ und nun Anno 1702 in den Druck gegeben worden.

Von
Daniel Falcknern/ Professore, Burgern und Pilgrim allda.

Franckfurt und Leipzig/
Zu finden bey Andreas Otto/ Buchhändlern.
Im Jahr Christi 1702.

had planted beyond the Atlantic. Nor was she mistaken in this. That German immigration has continued until this very hour, and the American continent from ocean to ocean bears the impress of German thrift, culture, progress and prosperity.

It is a wonderful story I have tried to tell. All history may be challenged to match it. There was unyielding resolution, determined perseverance, courage under the most adverse circumstances, a purpose that knew no shadow of turning, and a faith and a heroism that win our admiration and command our respect through all the years that have come and gone. These are the qualities that shine through all the trials and misadventures that befell these sturdy sons of the Fatherland.

The silver-tipped tongue of the orator, the pencil of the artist and the lyre of the poet cannot adequately tell the tale, and while the divine hand of Clio shall guide the eloquent pen of history, she will find no theme more worthy of her mission than this story of our ancestors, staking their all upon an uncertain venture into the New World. Bearing aloft that grand motto of their race, *Ohne Hast, ohne Rast*, they pressed onward toward the goal of their hopes with the same energy, determination and unflinching courage with which their ancestors seventeen centuries before had defied the power of Rome, and hurled back the legions of Cæsar.

APPENDIX.

A STREET CANAL IN ROTTERDAM.

APPENDICES.

Prefatory Note.

THERE are no surer nor safer guides for the chronicler of historical events, than the narratives to be found in contemporary records, especially when such records emanate from impartial sources and were never intended for publication. The carefully recorded minutes of a municipality or a Board of Administration endowed with executive functions, not only furnish a basis whereon the narrator may safely build, but they are at the same time certain to supply material not to be found elsewhere, thus becoming doubly valuable.

The unpublished records of the city of Rotterdam, and the Journal of the Proceedings of the English Commissioners for Promoting the Trade of the Kingdom, have been some of the sources from which part of the facts in the preceding narrative have been drawn. I have therefore thought it not without interest, if extracts from both these sources were given in this connection.

350 *The German Exodus to England in 1709.*

A great deal of other interesting material which could not properly be presented, either in the text or the notes, also accumulated on my hands, and I have utilized it here as throwing further light on the story of this Exodus.

APPENDIX A.

[A translation of some of the municipal records of the city of Rotterdam, and other documents, relating to the passage of the German emigrants through Holland, to England. From original copies obtained at Rotterdam and the Hague, by Julius F. Sachse, Esq., and now in the possession of the Historical Society of Pennsylvania. F. R. D.]

Extract from the Resolutions and Proceedings of the Burgomasters of Rotterdam:

ARMS OF ROTTERDAM.

APRIL 22, 1709, all of the Lords Burgomasters being present, it was resolved to pay over to Engel Kon and Samuel de Back, four hundred and fifty guilders, to be distributed among destitute families of the Lower Palatinate, for their subsistence on their journey, via England, to Pennsylvania, and a warrant shall be drawn.

April 29, 1709, all the Lords Burgomasters being present, it was resolved to pay over to Peter Toomen, a sum of three hundred guilders, for distribution among destitute families, who arrived after those heretofore

352   *The German Exodus to England in 1709.*

mentioned from the Lower Palatinate, for their subsistence as far as Pennsylvania, and a warrant shall be drawn.

A true copy.

UNGER,
Archivist of the City of Rotterdam.

An Extract from the Resolutions and Dispositions of Burgomasters:

Rec. 3.   Sheet 126, vol. 127.

PEOPLE COMING FROM THE PALATINATE TO GO TO ENGLAND.

August 12, 1709, all of the Lords Burgomasters being present, Mr. Joh. Steenhak excepted.

In consequence of a report of Hendrick Toren and Jan van Gent, concerning people from the Palatinate, already arrived and still to be expected, and others coming in great numbers from Germany, it was agreed to despatch eight notices, as follows:

"Burgomasters and Regents of the city of Rotterdam, hereby give notice, as a warning to the multitude of people who are coming over in great crowds from Germany, with the intention of being transported from here to England, and from there to Pennsylvania, and where they further may belong, that from exhibition of original letters and extracts and otherwise, it has appeared to Their Right Honorables, that Her Majesty of Great Britain has given orders not to send over any more of the said people to Her Majesty's charge, so long as those who are now in England have not been disposed of further. Their High Honorables give notice that Hendrick Toom and Jan van Gent, out of Christian charity and compassion, have taken pains, by order of her said Majesty, to provide for transportation and other necessities: that they are men of honor and perfect trustworthiness, and especially that in this case they have been requested and authorized, as they are again requested and authorized by these presents, to give and cause to be given notice hereof in such manner as they shall judge

Appendix A. 353

can properly and most effectually be done, to these of the Palatinate and others, who for the said purpose might intend to come over from Germany, thus preventing the said people from making a fruitless voyage to Holland. In witness whereof we have had some copies of these presents made and affixed thereto the seal of this city, and the signature of our Clerk, this 12 of August, 1709.

NOTE: August 24th, 1709. Present, the Lords Mar. Grolmna and Ads. Boosemele to the said Toom and Van Gent, who for eight days have been about with two yachts, one on the river Waal and the other on the river Maas, the sum of three hundred and fifty guilders is appropriated for their expenses, by ordinance of Burgomasters, as through the precaution taken by them, probably a thousand people who were on the road have gone back, so that according to all appearances those poor people shall be gotten rid of. And further the said Toom and Van Gent have been requested to take pains to travel up stream themselves in order to intercept those coming off with promise of indemnification of expenses in this case to be disbursed.

Extract from a letter sent to the Burgomasters of Rotterdam, by the Burgomasters and Regents of the city of Brielle. Pages 1707-1713, vol. 23.

RIGHT HONORABLE LORDS.

Among the people from the Palatinate, as well as from Hesse and other German quarters who have come down and are here lying in vessels at the pier, there are a great number who have not sufficient vituals to pursue their journey and many of whom are coming daily asking about their support, which for our small city is impossible, the poor pence being exhausted by the long continued support of soldiers' wives and children, whose husbands and fathers are in Spain; wherefore we pray your right Honorables to have the goodness to relieve the poverty of these indigent and suffering people, and to assist them, as we are unable to do so alone, and otherwise, in case of continuation, we would be obliged to send them back in boats to Rotterdam. We shall therefore hope that out of consideration your Right Honorables will not let them die of hunger and thirst, but lend a helping hand that these poor people may accomplish their intended journey.

Wherewith Right Honorable Lords we commend your Right Honorables to God's protection and remain

Your Right Honorables good friends
Burgomaster and Regents
of the city of Brielle.
By order of the same.
P. D. JAGEN.

BRIELLE, Aug. 24, 1709.

An extract from letter book No. 10 of the Burgomasters of Rotterdam:

TO THE VERY HONORABLE LORDS, BURGOMASTERS AND REGENTS OF THE CITY OF BRIELLE.

We can easily understand that your very Honorable City has to have much annoyance from people coming from Germany, but your very Honorables can also perceive therefrom how much greater the annoyance in this matter has been and still is for our city (even in proportion to the difference in population of both cities) for here has been and still is the first arrival, and it is here that orders, ships, convoy, wind and what not is waited for. The charity of our inhabitants towards these people is uncommon indeed, which certainly must reflect seriously on our own poor. Nevertheless, we have been obliged from time to time, to assist from the city treasury, so as to prevent calamities which might arise from the utter indigency of so large a crowd of people; and besides many sick and feble ones are in our city who remain to our charge. From all of which your Very Honorables will please pay some attention to it. We trust that your very Honorables shall reach the conclusion that in the whole country there is no city or place where the burden might be discharged with less reason than upon our city.

Moreover, these poor people have not the slightest relation to us whatever : wherefore we also have such complete confidence in your very Honorable's equity, that the same shall desist from the measures mentioned in their letter of the 24th, namely, the request of our assistance and much more, the sending of these poor people to our city. From the beginning we have applied all possible means on the one hand to transport those who had already arrived, in the quickest way possible, to England, and on the other hand to direct new arrivals as much as possible, both of which precautions have not only cost us much trouble but also much money, and we have especially at our expense, sent two merchants in two yachts up the rivers Waal and Teck which has had such effect that at least a thousand people have been diverted and that by their example others will likely change their mind. Without these precautions the hardships to your Honorable city would certainly have been much greater. If your Honorables wish to come and counsel with us about these measures, or about seeking help from the Government, we on our side will be prepared therefor, and we also will instruct on this subject, the Lords Deputies of this city to the assembly of their High Mightinesses. Therewith, very Honorable Lords, we recommend you to God's merciful protection.

Written at Rotterdam, this 26th of August, 1709. Your very Honorables' good friends, the

BURGOMASTERS AND REGENTS
of the city of Rotterdam.

Extract from the record of resolutions of the States General of the United Netherlands, 1709, vol. 2, fol. 348.

MONDAY, Sept. 16, 1709.
President, Lord Hocut. Present, Lord Van Welderen,

Van Oldersom, Pols, Van Essen, Niu Winckel, Menthen Hain, and the Extraordinary Deputy from the Province of Gelderland Hegcoop, Groenewegen, Van Waters, Van Dorp, Velders, Woorthey, Degm, Meerens, Grand Pensionary Heinsius, Harinxmotoe, Staten and Du Four.

The resolutions taken on the day before yesterday were called up. To the assembly was read a memorandum from Secretary Dayrolles, requesting that it may please their High Mightinesses to order the college of the Admiralty at Rotterdam, not to allow any more German families to be transported to England. The said memorandum to be inserted here, reading as follows:

"Whereupon, after deliberation, it has been decided to reply to the said Dayrolles that their High Mightinesses cannot prevent those families of the Palatines who already are in this country in order to cross over to England, from being taken thither, but that the Ministers at Cologne and Frankford shall be ordered to warn the people over there not to come this way for that purpose. And a copy of the aforesaid memorandum shall be

---

It affords me no little satisfaction that I am enabled to present a picture of the great gateway and wharf in Rotterdam, known as the HOOFD PORT, through which all these emigrants were compelled to pass, and from which, not only these Palatines, but the many thousands more who followed them into the New World, took shipping.

Situated on both sides of the river Maas, 19 miles from its mouth, and 45 miles from Amsterdam, Rotterdam has for centuries been one of the important seaports of Europe. The Rhine, of which the Maas is one of the outlets, gave Rotterdam easy water communication with many important German provinces, and the cantons of Switzerland, and it was at once the most direct as well as natural outlet to the sea, of all the emigrants from that quarter. Even at the present time, from 5000 to 20,000 persons sail annually from its wharfs to this country. For many decades most of the German emigrants took ship at Rotterdam, stopping, however at the little seaport of Cowes, on the isle of Wight, before finally setting sail for America.

This cut was made from an old, and very rare print in the possession of the Pennsylvania Historical Society, which has courteously permitted me to have a fac-simile taken.

THE HOOFD-POORT AT ROTTERDAM.
GATEWAY THROUGH WHICH ALL THE GERMAN EMIGRANTS PASSED TO THE WHARF FROM WHICH THEY SAILED FOR AMERICA.

Appendix A. 357

sent to the Presidents, Bilderheecks and Spina and they shall be directed that in case they should learn that more families from the Palatinate or elsewhere intend to come hither in order to cross over to England, to warn the same by such means as shall be deemed fittest, that they shall not be transported thither nor admitted into this country."

HIGH MIGHTY LORDS.

My Lords : I have had the honor the day before yesterday, to receive your High Mightinesses letter of the 16th inst, with a resolution of the same date attached, taken in pursuance of a memorandum of Secretary Dayrolles. In accordance with the order contained in said resolution, I shall by the fullest means cause all such people who I may learn will go from the Palatinate, or elsewhere, to Holland, in order to cross over to England, to be warned that they cannot be transported to England nor admitted in your High Mightinesses' country.
Tuesday last.

     High Mighty Lords
      Your High Mightinesses
       obedient and faithful servant,
        H. VAN BILDERHEECKS.

COLOGNE, Sep. 24, 1709.

HIGH MIGHTY LORDS.

My Lords ; Your High Mightinesses letter and resolution to the memorandum of the Secretary of Her Royal Majesty of Great Britain, taken on the 16th inst., I have with most humble respect duly received by the last mail. I shall not fail to comply therewith and by all fitting means warn such people as intend to go down stream.

But inasmuch as many Dutch Sailors some time since passed though this city to go down stream, who were deprived of everthing and the means which your High Mightinesses are wont to allow to their Ministers for the assistance of destitute ordinary travellers have been exhausted, I do not doubt but your High Mightinesses will have favorably reflected upon my proposition respectfully made to your High Mightinesses Clerk on the 8th inst. and honor me with their resolution, in order that these destitute people may not be left in need, in the severe winter season.

High Mighty Lords
Your High Mightinesses most humble
and most faithful servant,
P. DE SPINA,
Of Margroche.

FRANKFORT, Sept. 26, 1709.

APPENDIX B.

ARMS OF GREAT BRITAIN.

SEVERAL years ago a number of the friends of the Pennsylvania Historical Society raised a large sum of money, —$10,000 I believe— to have transcribed for the use of the Society, the complete manuscript minutes of the Public Record Office of England. These when completed will perhaps reach one hundred large volumes.

Fortunately for my purposes, the volumes covering the year 1709, reached this country while I was engaged in the preparation of this paper, and through the courtesy of Dr. Frederick D. Stone, the Society Librarian, they were placed at my service. Being the daily records of the Board, their accuracy is unimpeachable, and they have enabled me to correct inaccuracies in some of the other contemporary authorities I have consulted. The following extracts will seem to show how embarassing this

German immigration was to the English Government, and also the many schemes that were proposed to shake off the burden.

[F. R. D.]

Journal of the Proceedings of her Majesty's Commissioners for Promoting the trade of this Kingdom, and for inspecting and improving her Plantations in America and elsewhere.

(vol. 21)   WHITEHALL, May the 4th, 1709.

At a meeting of Her Majesty's Commissioners for Trade and Plantations.

Present:

Earl of Stamford.   Mr. Pulteney.
Sr. Ph. Meadows.   Mr. Moncton.

A letter from the Earl of Sunderland of Yesterday's Date, signifying that some hundreds of poor German Protestants are lately come, and that more are coming from the Palatinate to this Kingdom, and directing this Board to consider of a method for settling the said Germans in some part of this Kingdom, was read. Whereupon ordered that some of the Lutheran ministers in the Savoy have notice to attend the Board tomorrow morning.

WHITEHALL, May 5th, 1709.

Present:

Earl of Stamford.   Mr. Pulteney.
Sr. Ph. Meadows.   Mr. Moncton.

One of the Lutheran Ministers attending as directed yesterday, and being asked several questions in relation to poor German Protestants Mentioned in Yesterday's Minutes, He said that 300 men, women and children were already come over. That most of them were husbandmen and some few joyners and carpenters: that they are poor and have nothing to subsist on

Appendix B.

but what is given them in Charity, and are therefore threatened to be turned out of the house they are Lodged in; he added that there were 700 more of the said Poor Germans now at Rotterdam, who are expected over. And he promised to make a further Enquiry into the Circumstances of these Poor People and give their Lordships an answer thereof, in Writing as soon as Possible.

On May 6th, another letter from the Earl of Sunderland asking the Board to make full inquiry and directions given to write to the Lutheran Minister in the Savoy.

WHITEHALL, May 12th, 1709.

At a meeting of Her Majesty's Commissioners for Trade and Plantations.

Present:
Earl of Stamford.   Mr. Meadows.
            Mr. Moncton.

Monsieur Tribekko and Monsieur Ruperti, two of the Lutheran Ministers here, attending in relation to the Poor German Protestants, lately come from the Palatinate, mentioned in the minutes of the 5th instant. They presented to their Lordships, Memorials setting forth the Calamitous condition of these poor People, together with an account of their number, Amounting in all to 852 persons, men, women and children; their several Trades and Occupations, which were read. And these gentlemen being asked several questions thereupon, they said that several of them had died of want since their coming over. That they had no subsistence left. That they could not speak English, and that therefore none of them had as yet got any business or employment here, but possibly might do it in some time when they had learned the Language. Then being asked further what allowance they thought would be necessary for their present support until some provision could be otherwise made for them, They said they could not readily tell, But would withdraw and as near as Possible make a Calculation thereof;

and having done the same, they returned and proposed that sixteen pounds per day might be allowed the said 852 Persons for their present support and subsistence : Whereupon a letter to the Earl of Sunderland, signifying the same to his Lordship was drawn up and signed.

WHITEHALL, May the 16th, 1709.
At a meeting of Her Majesty's Commissioners for Trade and Plantations :
Present :
Earl of Stamford.   Sr. Ph. Meadows.
Mr. Moncton.

Mr. Ludolph and Justice Chamberlain attending, presented to their Lordships a Memorial, setting forth the reason of the Poor German Protestants coming over to this Kingdom, from the Palatinate, which being read, was returned to them again.

WHITEHALL, May 17th, 1709.
At a meeting of Her Majesty's Commissioners for Trade and Plantations.
Present :
Earl of Stamford.   Sr. Ph. Meadows.
Mr. Moncton.

A letter from the Earl of Sunderland of the 15th Instant (in answer to one writ to him on the 12th ditto) Signifying that Her Majesty had given orders for supplying the poor Germans as had been proposed in the said Letter, till they could be otherwise provided for, and that her Majesty was desirous to have the opinion of this Board how such Provision might be made for those Poor people &c was read. Whereupon their Lordships taking the same into consideration, and finding great difficulty in proposing a method to imploy them in such Manner as they may be able to support themselves here. A Letter to the

Plan of London and surrounding country immediately prior to the Exodus.

Appendix B.

Earl of Sunderland acquainting his Lordship therewith and desiring that he would give the Board an opportunity of Conferring with him on that Affair was signed.

Ordered that Mr. Tribekko and Mr. Ruperti, two of the Lutheran Ministers as likewise Mr. Chamberlain and Mr. Ludolph have notice to attend the Board to-morrow morning.

On the following day, May 18, Mr. Tribekko and Mr. Ruperti appeared before the Board. They said that the Tradesmen among them were able to work if they could but find employment. That the Husbandmen might also be provided for if they could but procure work. They believed all who were not sick were capable of working, but the Women and Children could do little else but Spin and Knit. Many of them were from the same county as those who had gone to New York, and were anxious to go there.[1]

At a meeting held on the 21st, Mr. Tribekko presented a list of such as could work. He said 200 of the men (most of them married) were able and fit to work and get a maintenance; that a Tailor and joiner had got into business; that 100 women could knit and spin and get a livelihood in that way. As to the rest, they were able to do but little, some being old and infirm; that they were now in pretty good condition, better accommodated than before.

On May 23, a list of the sick was presented to the Board. They (the Ministers) also gave the Board the unpleasant information that 1300 more of these Germans were come to the country but were still on shipboard, as no place could be found to lodge them. They also informed their Lordships that Her Majesty had been pleased to allow the first 852, £20 per day instead of £16.

---

[1] This allusion evidently refers to the colony led to New York in the previous year by Joshua von Kocherthal.

At a meeting of the Board on May 23, a memorial was presented from the United Governors, Assistants and Society of London for Mines Royal and Balley Works, proposing the employment of such of the poor Germans as are strong and able to labor in the Silver and Copper mines at Penlyn and Merionethshire.

WHITEHALL, May 24th, 1709.

At a meeting of Her Majesty's Commissioners for Trade and Plantations.

Present :

Earl of Stamford.   Sr. Ph. Meadows.
Lord Dartmouth.   Mr. Moncton.

A letter from Mr. Taylor inclosing a memorial relating to the Arrival of 1100 more German Protestants from the Palatinate, and that 600 more of them lie at Rotterdam for passage, signifying my Lord Treasurer's desire to know from this Board what is absolutely necessary as well for the 1100 already arrived as the 600 expected from Rotterdam, and how they may most properly be disposed of was read and directions given for Writing an Answer thereto.

Mr. Treke and Mr. Chamberlain attending in relation to the Said Poor People, they acquainted their Lordships that they were still on Shipboard at Woolwich, by reason they had no places provided for them to lodge in. That if tents could be procured, they would take care to Separate the said Germans and place some of them at Greenwich, Lambeth, Fulham and elsewhere, until they could find out work for them, which they hoped to do in a short time. Then being asked if the Ropeyard at Greenwich Should be repaired and fitted up, whether the same would not be convenient for their Accommodation for the present, till they should be otherwise taken care of. They said that the said Ropeyard would be very convenient for a great part of them. Whereupon these Gentlemen were told that their Lordships would give Directions for Writing this Morning to my Lord Treasurer to acquaint him herewith.

Appendix B.

May 25, Mr. Tribekko presented a new list to the Board, containing the names of such as were able to work, and such as were not either from Age or Sickness. It contained only 806 names. He said five or six and twenty have died since their arrival. He proposed that £100 should be laid out for flax, iron and steel that the women might be set to spinning and the men employed in making tools for husbandry.

On May 30, the Board instructed the Solicitor General to advise them whether Her Majesty had the right and power to grant parcels of land in her Forests, Chases and Waters in order to convert them to tillage, and also what Security Her Majesty may give to indemnify Parishes for introducing poor families among them.

On June 3, Inquiry was made as to the character of the Society of London for Royal Mines.

WHITEHALL, June 7th, 1709.

At a meeting of Her Majesty's Commissioners for Trade and Plantations.

Present:

Lord Dartmouth.   Sr. Ph. Meadows.
Mr. Moncton.

Mr. Tribekko attending informed their Lordships that 2000 more Poor People were Arrived from the Palatinate in Germany, whereupon he was acquainted that it would be proper for him to present a memorial thereof to a Secretary of State, which he Promised to do accordingly.

Dr. Stringer attended and informed the Lords that the Society (of London for Mines Royal) was incorporated by Queen Elizabeth in the 10th year of her reign. He was requested to produce the seal of incorporation.

WHITEHALL, June 15th, 1709.

At a meeting of Her Majesty's Commissioners for Trade and Plantations.

Present:
Lord Dartmouth.   Sr. Ph. Meadows.
Mr. Moncton.

The proposal of Lord Chamberlain for settling some of the Palatines in Staffordshire and Gloucestershire was considered. He had great parcels of land in these counties which were waste of which he could grant to each family a sufficient amount for the term of three years, they paying a penny an acre. That he would at once take 20 or 25 families. That they should have timber and lime with the lands for building, but he hoped the Queen would be at the charge of erecting the cottages and subsist them until they were in a condition to help themselves.

On the 21 fresh proposals were considered from Lord Chamberlain. They declined his offer and said to accept of it and settle all the Germans would cost £150.000. That the idea was not to put them on a better footing than British subjects, but merely to aid them until they could help themselves. These Settlers would benefit his Lordship's estate, as he could retain them as tenants. Her Majesty could only be at the charge of conveying them there.

On June 23, Mr. Tribekko presented a memorial to the Board that there had been a great increase in the number of the Palatines, and they could not be taken care of without greater assistance, and asking for the same.

A memorial was also read from Dr. Stringer and others about employing the Palatines in some mines in Wales and elsewhere.

A warrant from her Majesty dated June 4, 1709, calling for £24 daily to the Germans was over and above the £16 per day, was read. Also another of the 14th calling for the payment of £40 daily.

A proposal was made to settle 200 families in the island of Jamaica, but the planters objected, as they were required to send some of their negroes to make a preparatory settlement for the Germans.

Appendix B. 367

On August 8th, the Board discussed the speedy settlement of the Palatines so as to put an end to the heavy expense of their subsistence. It was resolved to give special encouragement to persons and parishes as should be willing to receive any of these poor Palatines. It was agreed to allow each parish £5 per head for such care, the Queen to be at the charge of sending them to their respective places.

On August 17th, Colonel Laws advocated before the Board, the sending of a colony of Germans to Jamaica. There were, he said, 40,000 negroes there and not above 2,500 whites. There was much unsettled land, enough for 50,000 families.

This Jamaica Settlement was discussed at almost every meeting of the Board but nothing ever came of it.

Lord Carbury also had great tracts of lands on which he offered to colonize some of the Germans, but he asked £5 per acre which was deemed excessive. Later however, he made a more liberal offer which was discussed at further meetings of the Board, but there is no record that any ultimate arrangement of this kind was made with him.[2]

[2] Records of the Board of Trade.

APPENDIX C.

A Brief for the Collection of Money Asked for, and Granted by the Queen.

TO THE QUEEN'S MOST EXCELLENT MAJESTY.

ARMS OF CHUR-SACHSEN.

THE Humble Petition of your Majesties, Justices of Peace for the County of Middlesex, held at Hick's Hall, June 7, 1709

Showeth,

That being inform'd that several Thousand *Germans* of the *Protestant* Religion, oppressed by Exactions of the *French* in their own Country, have fled for Refuge into this your Majesty's Kingdom of *Great Britain*; who must have perished, had not your Majestie's Generous and Seasonable Bounty subsisted them; and being sensible that they labor still under great Wants, and stand in need of farther Relief for their Subsistence, do therefore crave leave to offer your Majesty our Humble Opinion, That a

Appendix C.

Brief for the Collection of the Charity of all well disposed Persons, in all Churches and Meetings, and otherwise within this County, as soon as your Majesty shall think fit to grant it; will be effectual to Raise a considerable Sum for their present Relief. All of which we Humbly submit to your Majesties great Wisdom; and we shall, as in Duty bound, ever Pray.

AT THE COURT OF ST. JAMES'S, JUNE 16, 1709. PRESENT THE QUEEN'S MOST EXCELLENT MAJESTY IN COUNCIL.

Upon Reading this Day at the Board the Humble Petition of the Justices of Peace for the County of *Middlesex*, at the general Sessions of Peace for the said County; representing to her Majesty, the great Wants and Necessities of several Thousand *Germans* of the *Protestant* Religion, who being oppressed by the Exactions of the *French* in their own Country, have fled for Refuge into this Kingdom, and must have perished, had not her Majesty's Generous and Seasonable Bounty reliev'd them: And humbly offering that for their further Relief and subsistence, a Brief may be Issued for the Collection of the Charity of well disposed Persons within the said County. Her Majesty out of her tender Regard and Compassion to these Poor People, is pleased to condescend thereunto, and to order that the Right Honorable, the Lord High Chancellor of Great Britain do cause Letters Patents to be prepared, and passed under the Great Seal for that Purpose, &c.

Accordingly, a Brief has been Granted by Her Majesty for the Relief, Subsistence and Settlement of the Poor Distressed *Palatines*, to this Effect.

THE BRIEF.

Whereas by reason of the many great Hardships and Oppressions which the People of the Palatinate, near the Rhine, in Germany, (more especially the Protestants) have sustained and lain under for several Years past, by the frequent Invasions and repeated Inroads of the French, (whereby more than Two

Thousand of their greatest Cities, Market Towns and Villages) have been burnt down to the Ground; as Heidelburg, Manheim, Worms, Spire, Frankendale, and other Towns; and great Numbers have perished in Woods, and Caves, by Hunger, Cold and Nakedness, Several Thousands have been forced to leave their Native Country, and seek Refuge in other Nations; and of them near Eight Thousand Men, Women and Children, are come, and are now in and near the City of London, in a very poor and miserable Condition. And whereas it hath been humbly Represented unto us, as well by an Address of our Justices of the Peace for the County of Middlesex, at their General Session of the Peace, held at Hick's Hall as by others (of) our Loving Subjects, on the behalf of the said Poor Palatines: That Notwithstanding our Bounty allowed to them, without which they must have perished; yet they still labor under great wants, and stand in need of further Relief for their Subsistence and Settlement, in such manner that they may not only support themselves, but be rendered capable of Advancing the Wealth and Strength of our Nation, in regard they are naturally of a strong, healthful Constitution, inur'd to Labor and Industry, and great part of them to Husbandry; therefore the said Justices, and our other Loving Subjects, on behalf of the said Poor Distressed Palatines, have humbly besought us to Grant unto the said Poor Palatines, our Gracious Letters Patents, License and Protection, under our Great Seal of Great Britain, to impower them to Ask, Collect and Receive, the Alms and Benevolence of all our Loving Subjects, throughout that part of our Kingdom of Great Britain called England, Dominion of Wales and Town of Berwick upon Tweed, UNTO which humble Request we have Graciously condescended, not doubting but when these Presents shall be made known unto our Loving Subjects, they will readily and cheerfully contribute to the Relief and Support of the said poor Distressed Palatines: considering them as Brethren, and Sympathizing with them in this their Miserable State and Condition.

Appendix C.

KNOW YE THEREFORE, that of our Special Grace and Princely Compassion, we have Given and Granted to the said poor Palatines, and to their Deputy or Deputies, the Bearer and Bearers thereof: full Power, License and authority to Ask, Collect and Receive the Alms and Charitable Benevolence of our Loving Subjects; Not only Householders, but also Servants, Strangers, Lodgers, and others in all the Cities, Towns, Villages, &c., In our kingdom of England, &c. We likewise purposing to cause the like License and Authority to be granted in Relation to our Loving Subjects in Scotland. And we do require all Parsons, Vicars, Curates, Teachers and Preachers of every Separate Congregation, to read the said Brief in their Several Churches and Congregations, and earnestly to exhort their Auditors to a liberal Contribution of their Charity to the said Poor Palatines: and that the Minister and Church Warden of every Parish, shall go from House to House to Ask and Receive from their Parishioners their Christian and Charitable Contributions.

And we do hereby Authorize and Appoint the Lord Archbishop of Canterbury, the Lord High Chancellor, Lord High Treasurer, &c. (with a great number of our Lords Spiritual and Temporal, Knights, Gentlemen, &c.,) To be Trustees and Receivers of the said Charity, &c. And to dispose and Distribute the Money which shall be Collected, in such manner as shall be found Necessary and Convenient for the better Employment and Settlement of the said Poor Palatines, by making Contracts in their behalf or by any other Lawful Means and Ways whatsoever, &c.

In Pursuance of this Brief the Following Order was Published:

WHITE HALL, July 20th, 1709.

By Order of the Right Honorable, the Lords and others, her Majesties Commissioners for Receiving and Disposing of the Money to be Collected for the Subsistence and Settlement of the poor Palatines: Notice is hereby given, that they will hold their General Meeting at Doctors Commons every Wednesday at Four in the Afternoon. Notice is hereby likewise given, that the said Commissioners are come to a Resolution for disposing and settling as many of the said Palatines as conveniently they can, in North Britain and Ireland, and the Plantations, and that they will at their Committee receive Proposals in order thereunto.

Notice is likewise given, that any Masters of Ships, Trading in the coal, or other Coast Trade, are at liberty to employ such of the said Palatines, as are willing to serve them on Board such ships; and that such Masters may apply themselves to a Person Appointed to attend at the several Places where the said Palatines now are for that Purpose.[3]

The Persons appointed Commissioners and Trustees by the said Letters Patent, were:

The Lord Archbishop of Canterbury.
Lord High Chancellor of Great Britain.
Lord High Treasurer of Great Britain.
John, Lord Somers, Lord President of the Council.
John, Duke of Newcastle, Lord Privy Seal.
William, Duke of Devonshire, Steward of the Household.
Charles, Duke of Somerset, Master of the Horse.
James, Duke of Ormund.
Wriothesly, Duke of Bedford.
John, Duke of Buckingham and Normandy.
James, Duke of Queensbury and Dover, Secretary of State.
Henry, Marquis of Kent, Chamberlain of the Household.
Evelyn, Marquis of Dorchester.
Thomas, Earl of Pembroke and Montgomery, Lord High Admiral of Great Britain.
James, Earl of Derby.
Thomas, Earl of Stamford.

---

[3] State of the Palatines.

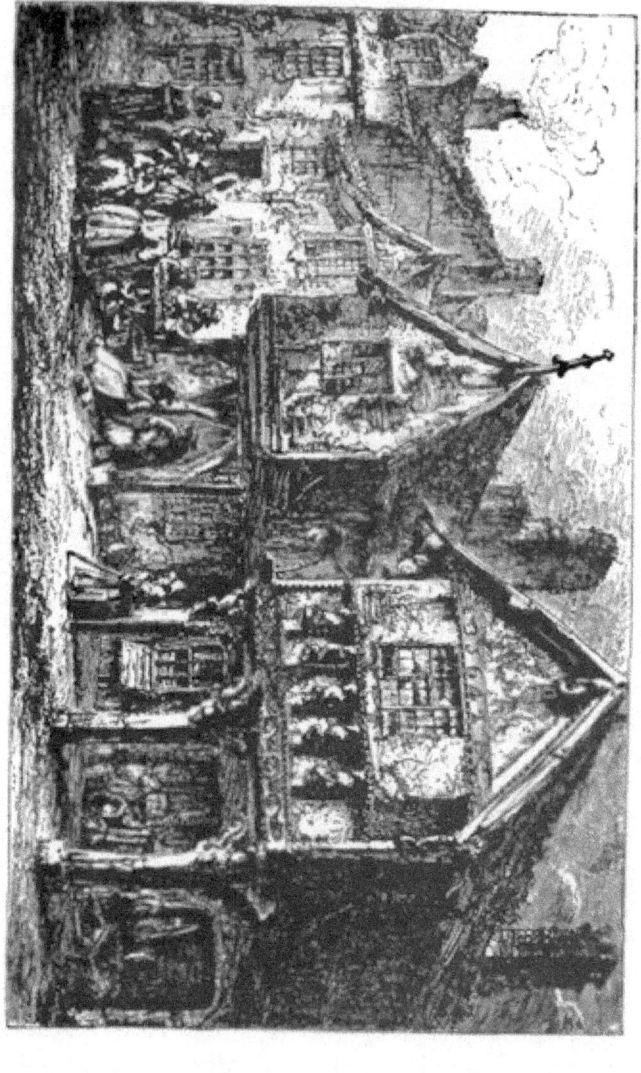

A STREET SCENE IN LONDON IN 1709.
FROM A CONTEMPORARY PRINT.

Appendix C.

Charles, Earl of Sunderland, Secretary of State.
Lawrence, Earl of Rochester.
Henry, Lord Bishop of London.
Thomas, Lord Bishop of Rochester.
Jonathan, Lord Bishop of Winchester.
John, Lord Bishop of Ely.
William, Lord Bishop of Lincoln.
William, Lord Dartmouth.
Charles, Lord Halifax.
The Right Honorable Mr. Secretary Boyle.
James Vernon, Esq.
Lord Chief Justice Holt.
Sir John Trevor, Master of the Rolls.
Lord Chief Justice Trevor.
Sir Charles Hedges.
John Smith, Esq., Chancellor of the Exchequer.
Sir James Montague, Knight, Attorney General.
Robert Eyre, Esq., Solicitor General.
The Lord Mayor, Aldermen, Recorder, and Sheriffs of the city of London.
The Honorable Spencer Compton, Esq.
The Honorable George Watson, Esq.
Sir Matthew Dudley.
Sir John Bucknall.
Sir John Stanley.
Sir Henry Furnace.
Sir John Phillips, Bart.
Sir Alexander Cairns, Bart.
Sir Theodore Janssen.
Sir James Collett.
Sir Edmund Harrison.
Sir William Scawen, Knight.
Sir John Elwill, Knight.
Dr. Willis, Dean of Lincoln.
Dr. White Kennet, Dean of Peterborough.
Dr. ——Godolphin, Dean of St. Pauls.

Dr. Thomas Manningham, Dean of Windsor.
Dr. Thomas Bray.
Dr. George Smallridge.
Dr. Moss.
Dr. Bradford.
Dr. Butler.
Dr. Linford.
Dr. Pelling.
The Rev. Samuel Clerk.
Conradus Wornley.
Ulrich Scherer.
John Tribekko and Andrew Ruperty, Clerks.
Samuel Travers, Esq., Surveyor General.
John Plumer.
John Shute.
Joseph Offley.
Richard Walaston.
David Hexsteter.
John Ward.
Henry Cornish.
Nathaniel Gould.
Justus Beck.
John Dolben.
Richard Marten.
Arthur Bailey.
Micaija Perry.
Henry Martin.
William Dudley.
George Townsend.
Thomas Railton.
Ralph Bucknal.
John Chamberlayne.
William Dawson, Esq.
Francis Eyles, Esq.
Frederick Slare, Doctor of Physic.
James Keith, Doctor of Physic.

Appendix C.

Thomas Smith, Esq.
Robert Hales.
Henry William Ludolph.
Robert de Neuvillic.
Peter Foy.
William Falkener.
Henry Hoar.
Walter Cock, Gent.
Jonathan James, Gent.[4]

---

[4] Palatine Refugees in England, pp. 35-36.

APPENDIX D.

[The passage of a Naturalization act by Great Britain early in the Spring of 1709, was not lost upon Holland. That country had been benefitted to an almost inconceivable degree by the Huguenot refugees who were driven out of France by the revocation of the Edict of Nantes, many of whom had settled themselves in the Low Countries. When, therefore, Holland again saw these thousands of industrious men, farmers and handicraftmen, invited to become citizens of Great Britain, she also passed a naturalization act in the hope they might be induced to tarry in the Netherlands. The following is the proclamation which was issued on June 24, 1709, by the States of Holland and West Friesland, for the general naturalization of Protestants.   F. R. D.]

HOLLAND'S NATURALIZATION ACT.

ARMS OF AMSTERDAM.

THE States of Holland and West Friesland, to all who shall hear and see these Presents, Greeting : We make it known that having taken into consideration that the Grandeur and Prosperity of a country does not in general consist of the Multitude of Inhabitants and that in particular this Prince is increased in Power and Riches by the Concourse of unhappy and dispersed Persons,

A VIEW IN HOLLAND.

who being driven from their own Country for the Profession of the True Reformed Religion, or other oppressions, have taken sanctity in this Province, and have a long time since contributed to the increase of Trade and Public Wealth. That beside the Refugees, who left France upon account of their Religion and have already lived a considerable time in this Country, have rendered themselves worthy of the favorable attention of the Regency for their Persons and Families, and consequently ought to enjoy their General Protection as the other Inhabitants.

For these causes We have thought fit to Order and Decree as we Order and Decree by these Presents, that all persons who have withdrawn themselves out of the Kindgom of France, or other Countries, for the Profession of the true Reformed Religion, and have taken Sanctuary in this Province of Holland and West Friesland, and settled themselves therein, and likewise the Children of the said persons whom they brought with them, or were born in the Said Province, as also all other such Refugees, who for the future shall either directly out of France or other Countries, take Refuge in this Province and close their Abode therein shall be received and acknowledged, as we do receive and acknowledge them by these Presents, for our Subjects, and Natives of our country of Holland and West Friesland, and by virtue thereof shall enjoy for the future Privilege and Prerogatives that our other Natural Born Subjects enjoy, as such of them belonging; and that in consequence thereof they shall enjoy the Rights of Naturalization according to the Resolution bearing the date of Sept. 25, 1670. That therefore all these who will take the Benefit of this our Favor shall apply personally to the President or Commissioner of the Court ; under whose jurisdiction they are, or to Magistrates or Town Baliffs and Judges of Villages where they are settled, or intend to chose their Abode, who after a short Examination, to know whether the Said Persons are truly Refugees, as aforesaid, shall Register their Names, that the same may appear forever. And that this may be known to everybody, we require these presents to be Published and Affixed and Executed in the usual manner.

Done at the Hague, July 18, 1709.

SIMON VAN BEAUMONT.

APPENDIX E.

THE PALATINATE.

BRIEF SKETCH OF THE POLITICAL HISTORY OF THE COUNTRY FROM THE ELEVENTH TO THE EIGHTEENTH CENTURY, DRAWN FROM VARIOUS SOURCES.

[Few names are more familiar to persons of average culture than *The Palatinate*, used in a geographical sense. Every one of German origin has heard it repeated again and again as a household term, and yet how many, even among those who are reckoned as scholarly men know more about it than that it was a German province and famous for the sufferings of its people during the seventeenth century, as the varying fortunes of war made them the victims alike of victor and vanquished? Inasmuch as by far the greatest number of those who went to England in 1709 came from the Palatinate, and as it was for more than half a century afterward one of the main sources of the German emigration to Pennsylvania, a more general account of this historic land will not be inappropriate here. F. R. D.]

ARMS OF THE CHUR-PFALTZ.

THE two territorial divisions known as the Upper and Lower Palatinate, had a separate existence as early as the 11th century. At that time they, along with the duchy of Souabia, the duchy of Franconia, the palatinate of Burgundy west of Mount Jura, the province of Egra and other fiefs in Switzerland, the Tyrol and elsewhere, composed the possessions of the imperial dynasty of Hohenstaufen, which took its name from a high conical mountain—*der hohe Staufen*—in the valley of the Rems, in Soubia. There Frederick of Büren, the founder of the family, had built a mighty castle, the home of his chivalrous race. He married Agnes, daughter of Henry IV, Emperor of Germany, and she brought him the duchy of Soubia as a dower. For nearly 200 years the Hohenstaufens held sway. The last of the name, Conradin, wasted his heritage in his Italian campaigns and perished on the scaffold at Naples in 1268. The duchy of Franconia was dismembered. This Palatinate which formed a part of it fell into the hands of new owners.

The Palatinate comprised two separate provinces, which were divided from each other by the secular and ecclesiastical state of Franconia. First was the Palatinate on the Rhine, or Lower Palatinate—*Pfalz am Rhein*—situated on both sides of that River, and bounded by Würtemburg, Baden, Alsace, Lorraine, Treves and Hesse. It contained 2288 square miles and to-day contains about 700,000 inhabitants. The Upper Palatinate, or *Ober-Pfalz* on the east was surrounded by Bohemia, Bavaria and Nurnburg. The Upper Palatinate contains 3845 square miles and about 550,000 souls.

The Emperor Frederick II gave the Palatinate to Louis of Bavaria and it remained a part of that country until 1329, when the Emperor Louis IV in the treaty of Pavia conferred it on the sons and relatives of his brother. The Electoral dignity was alternately exercised by the Duke of Bavaria and the holders of the Rheinish Palatinate, because the electoral dignity was attached to the Rhein Pfalz, whose court was invested with the judiciary power of the empire in case of the absence of the Emperor. Though divided into four lines, the Palatinate was nevertheless considered as a united State. These lines were as follows : First the Electorate on the Rhine,—*Kur-Rhein*. Second, Sulzbach, or *Upper Palatinate*, established by Count John. Third, Simmern, with the counties of Veldenz and

Appendix E.

Spa heim, on the Rhine, north of the Electorate. Fourth, Mossbach, on the Neckar, in Souabia.

In the Golden Bull issued by the Emperor Charles IV, in 1356, all the rights and privileges which the great vassals of the empire had usurped, were conceded to them. The electors were seven in number, ranking in the following order : I. the Archbishop of Mayence, as Arch Chancellor of Germany, II. the Archbishop of Treves, as Arch Chancellor of Burgundy. III. the Archbishop of Cologne, as Arch Chancellor of Italy. IV. The King of Bohemia, as Arch Seneschal. V. the Count Palatine, as Arch-Sewer, VI. the Duke of Saxe Wittenberg as Arch Marshal, and VII. the Margrave of Brandenburg. These territories were considered inalienable feudal possessions of the Empire.

Coming down to a more recent period we find the electorate in the hands of Frederick III, in 1559, who introduced Calvinism, and gave his protection to the Huguenots. He maintained the Reformed religion with extreme severity throughout his electorate. Sylvan, a Socinian clergyman who would admit of but one person in the Godhead, was beheaded by his order in 1572. His son Louis, who was a zealous Lutheran, tried to undo all his father's work. On entering his Capital, Heidelberg, he ordered all of his subjects who were not Lutherans to leave the city. The Calvinist preachers who refused to recant, were expelled the country. From this time on the people of the Palatinate were frequently compelled to change their religion to comform with the tenets of the ruling princes, being successively Catholic, Calvinistic, Lutheran, Calvinistic and again Lutheran.

Ludevick V lost his electorate in 1623 to his kinsman the Duke of Bavaria. The latter retained the Upper Palatinate and the electoral dignity, but in 1648 the Rheinish Palatinate was conveyed to Frederick's son, and the VIII. electorate created for him. During the war of the Spanish Succession, in 1694, the Elector again revived the Upper Palatinate, and all the ancient rights resumed again by Bavaria after the war. During these numerous changes the Palatinate was cruelly desolated by the armies that from motives of conquest and religion overran her soil. In 1801 France seized all on the west bank of the Rhine, and divided the remainder between Bavaria, Nassau and Hesse Darmstadt. In 1815 the left bank was restored to Germany, the greater part of the Lower Palatinate being given to Bavaria; Prussia got the Rhine Province, Hesse Starkenburg and Rhine Hesse, while Baden received Manheim, Heidelberg and Mossback.[4a]

OFFICIAL TITLES OF THE ELECTOR.[5]

The Elector Palatine's titles are: By the Grace of God, Count Palatine of the Rhine, Arch-Treasurer and Elector of the Empire, Duke of Bavaria, Juliers, Cleves and Berg; Count of Veldentz, Spanheim, Marck, Ravensburg and Mœurs, Lord of Ravenstein, &c., &c.

Frederick the IV marry'd Louisa Julia of Orange, had great quarrels with the House of Austria about Religion and dy'd Anno Dom 1610. His Son and Successor, Frederick the Vth. marry'd Elizabeth, Daughter of James the Ist, of Great Britain. Succeeded to his Fathers Quarrels with the House of Austria about Religion, and was chosen King of Bohemia; but for want of being duly supported, was defeated at the Battel of Prague; after which he lost both his Crown and his Dominions. He had Issue the illustrious Princess *Sophia*, born in 1630; marry'd *Earnest Augustus*, Duke of *Hanover*, who is now Electress Dowager, Mother to the present Elector, presumptive Heiress to the Crowns of *Great Britain* and *Ireland*, and as

---

[4a] The principal authorities consulted in preparing this brief sketch were *Koeppen's Middle Ages, Chambers Cyclopedia* and *Menzel's Germany*.

[5] Palatine Refugees in England, p. 21.

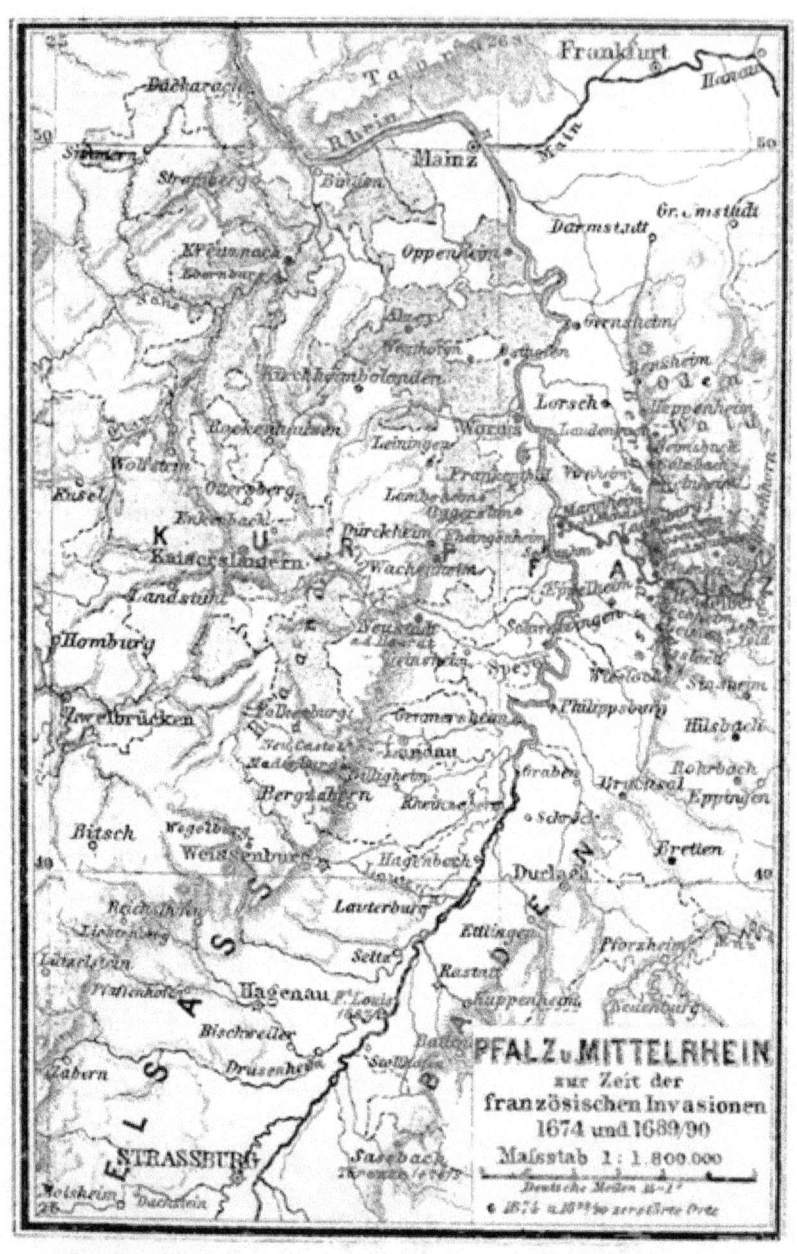

Map of the Palatinate at the close of the 17th Century.

illustrious for her excellent Qualities, as for her high birth. [6] *Frederick* the V was succeeded by his Son, *Charles Louis*, who by the Treaty of Westphalia was restor'd to the Lower Palatinate, and the Electoral Dignity. He was a pious and learned Prince, and dy'd in 1680. His son *Charles* succeeded, was Elector of this Line, and dy'd without Issue in 1685. The present Elector is (by failure of the fore-mention'd Line) of the Branch of *Newburgh*, of the Family of *Deux Ponts*. The Majority of the People are Protestants, who have been much discourag'd since the Succession of the Duke of *Newburgh*, a Papist, to the Electorate, and by the *barbarous* Invasions of the French.[7]

ANOTHER ACCOUNT OF THE PALATINATE AND ITS RULERS, TOGETHER WITH SOME OF ITS POLITICAL VICISSITUDES IN THE LATTER HALF OF THE SEVENTEENTH CENTURY.

The Poor Palatines who are the objects of our present Charity, inhabited lately a Principality in Germany called the Palatinate, which is divided into the Upper and Lower Palatinate: the Upper belonging to the Duke of Bavaria, according to the Treaty of Munster and the Lower to the Count Palatine of the Rhine, who formerly enjoyed the whole. The Countrey takes its name from the Office of Count Palatine, bestowed by the Emperor on those who administered Justice in his Name to the Empire; of which there were two, one on the Rhine, who had the Charge of Franconia, and the neighboring Countreys, and the other in Saxony and other Countreys subject to the Saxony law. Hence it is that the Electors of Saxony and

---

[6] Sophia, the granddaughter of James I, the youngest of thirteen children, was born on October 13, 1630. As stated above she was declared by Parliament to be entitled to the succession after the death of Queen Anne. She did not attain the crown. She died on June 8, 1714. She was the mother of George I. who was proclaimed King of Great Britain immediately upon the death of Queen Anne on August 1, 1714.

[7] Palatine Refugees in England, pp. 21-22.

the Elector Palatine or the Elector of Bavaria are Vicars of the Empire in their respective Provinces, when there is an interregnum by the Emperor's death or otherwise. At first the Count Valentine of the Rhine had no possessions on that River, but in Process of Time, got them by Marriage, Purchase or Imperial Gift, and formed a very considerable Principality. In 1576 the Elector Frederick III began to entertain many Protestant Families at Frankendale, who fled from the Low Countries. His Successors doing the like in other Towns, did thereby mightily enrich that Country. This Prince made his Revenue very considerable by taking away the Church Lands upon the Change of Religion; by his Right of conducting Strangers whom he obliged to make use of his Guards, not only in his own Territories, but in the neighboring Bishopricks, and Earldoms, and by Toll upon Merchandize that passes his Dominions, and the Title he has to the Goods of Strangers, or of those who came to Settle without express leave, in the Palatinate.

Frederick III was succeeded by his son, Lewis IV, who turned Protestant, and was succeeded by Frederick IV, who abandoned Popery. He married Louise, daughter of the Prince of Orange, by whom he had Frederick V, who was chosen King of Bohemia, but who by the loss of a great Battle at Prague, and the Supineness of the English Court, who ought to have assisted him, he marrying Elizabeth, Daughter to King James I, he was obliged to abandon his Countrey. He died at Mentz in 1632, leaving him Three Sons, Charles, Lewis, Robert or Rupert, and Edward. Prince Rupert lived in England, and died without Legitimate Issue. Edward left Three Daughters; one named Sophia, married to the Duke of Hanover, and is now alive, and declared by act of Parliament the next Protestant Succession to the Crown of England, after the Decease of our Most Gracious Queen Anne, whom God grant long to Reign. Charles succeeded his Father Frederick V in the Electorate Palatine, and married Charlotte, Daughter of the Landgrave of Hesse Castle, by whom he had Charles and Elizabeth Charlott. She was married to the Duke of Orleans, only Brother to the

Appendix E.

present French King, (Louis XIV) in 1687. It was reported at that time that King Louis having by Treaty of Marriage allowed that Princess, who was a Protestant, the Liberty to use her own Religion, yet when she came to the Frontiers of that Kingdom, on her way to Paris, to consummate her Marriage, that faithless King sent her a Peremptory Message that she should proceed no farther unless she would renounce the Protestant Religion. Whereupon the unhappy Prince, her Father, who was afraid to incur his Anger, consented thereto[8] to save his Dominions from Destruction ; but in a Year or Two after upon some unjust Pretence, he sent the Dauphin, his Son, with a great Army into that Countrey, who ruined it in the most Deplorable Manner that was ever heard of.

Charles succeeded his Father in the Electorate, and William, Duke of Newburg, a Roman Catholic, is the present Elector Palatine.

To show how the Palatinate was overrun by the fierce Soldiery of different nations the following brief statement may be quoted :

The City of Philipsburg, reckon'd the first in the Palatinate, has been taken six times ; viz. in 1633, by the Imperialists, the Year After by the Swedes, and in 1636, by the Imperialists, in 1644 by the Duke d' Enghien, afterwards Prince of Conde, by the Germans in 1676, and by the Dauphin on his Birth Day, the 1st of November, 1688, but was restor'd to the Empire by the Treaty of Ryswick.[9]

---

[8] State of the Palatines, pp. 3-4.
[9] Palatine Refugees in England, p. 26.

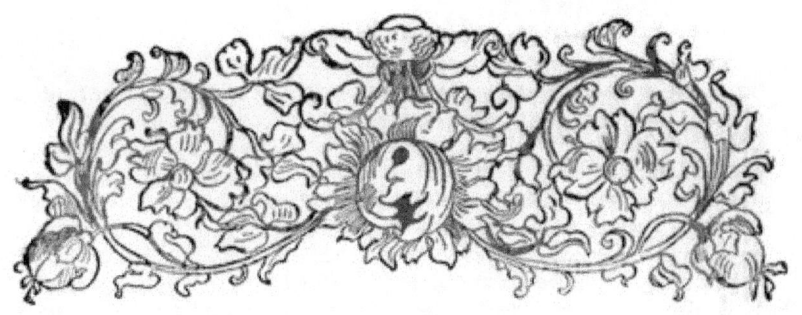

APPENDIX F.

ARMS OF PENN, FROM THE FIRST PROVINCIAL CURRENCY PRINTED 1723.

I AVAIL myself of this opportunity to express my sincere thanks to my good friend, Hon. Samuel W. Pennypacker, of the Philadelphia Court of Common Pleas, for the loan of an extremely rare and most curious and valuable little book, published in 1711, a fac-simile of the title-page of which is reproduced on page 389. Chapter VI of this rare volume gives what purports to be a detailed account of the exact number of these German emigrants, their daily life in London and elsewhere in England, their places of residence, the regulations of their several camps, their treatment by the English Government and populace, the efforts to settle them throughout the United Kingdoms and elsewhere and their final disposition. So interesting have I found all these details that I have translated the entire chapter and present it herewith.

The name of the writer of this account is, I believe, unknown; but whoever he may have been, and his barbarous German does not indicate a man of much culture, he evidently was personally on the spot at the time, and had actual knowledge of much that he relates. There is no reason to doubt so much of his narrative as came under his own observation; but my investigations among other and as I believe unquestionable contemporary sources of information have satisfied me that he greatly although unintentionally no doubt, exaggerates the number of these German arrivals. The amount of money raised by public subscriptions, and the sums appropriated from time to time from the English Treasury and applied to the relief of these strangers are on record. It is also in evidence among how many persons these monies were distributed. The number does not reach one half those given by our author. Official documents must be given credence as against the statements of a narrator who presents us with his unsupported account only. In fact, another writer, a contemporary, whose account is printed in this same book and next to this account, sets down the number at less than one half that given in this chapter. It also is very specific, and pretends to give even the nationality of all these emigrants. It will be found in Appendix H.

I incline to the opinion that this is the original source of the statement that these Germans in London, in 1709, numbered more than 33,000 souls, found in Löher, Rupp, Fisher and other writers, all of whom have made the assertion without indicating the sources of their information. Löher was perhaps the first to copy it, and all the rest followed him blindly. This unknown writer's narrative is, however, the fullest and most minute of any I have found, and is marvelously interesting despite his uneven temper and frequent contradictory statements. I may add that I believe this is the first time this narrative has been given to the public in the English language.

F. R. D.

388   *The German Exodus to England in 1709.*

CHAPTER VI.

"BEING A SHORT ACCOUNT OF THOSE GERMANS WHO, AS IT WERE THROUGH SOME SPECIES OF ENCHANTMENT, IN 1709, SAILED OVER THE SEA INTO ENGLAND. HOW IT FARED WITH THEM, WHEN THEY ARRIVED AND WHERE THEY AFTERWARDS TOOK UP THEIR ABODE."

HANSEATIC ARMS.
(LONDON.)

IN order not to detain the courteous reader with a tedious and unpleasant narration, I will briefly refer to the things which were done openly in England, before the "Præludia," before the arrival of the Germans in 1708, on Blackheath. On the 24-25-26-27 and 28 days of July, 1708, not only in the gloomy night, but also in broad daylight, many things were witnessed by all four camps whereon the following year, the Germans camped on the Black Head or "Blackheath," namely upon the Ritter-Kamm, and in the "Camberwell," and in the Middle camp, just like a well laid off military encampment, many thousands of people, of divers kinds, and religiously educated, saw the spectacle with their own eyes, and to which they have solemnly attested, and have related to the minutest details, all the circumstances worthy of belief.

Among others, there was one witness, deep rooted in the faith, Jaun Alplin, minister of Capella College, near Grinovium, and also Mr. John Burian, minister in the church of Dertforth, not yet knowing what significance should come out of this. In appearance, it has become cause for higher admiration and

Appendix F.

Das verlangte / nicht erlangte Canaan bey den Lust-Gräbern;

Oder Ausführliche Beschreibung

Von der unglücklichen Reise derer jüngsthin aus Teutschland nach dem Engelländischen in America gelegenen

Carolina und Pensylvanien

wallenden Pilgrim / absonderlich dem einseitigen übelgegründeten

Kochenthalersschen Bericht

wohlbedächtig entgegen gesetzt

In

I. Einem Beantwortungs-Schreiben etlicher diese Sach angehenden Fragen; nebst einer Vorrede Moritz Wilhelm Höens.

II. Ermahnungs-Schreiben an die bereits dahin verreißte Teutsche / Anthon Wilhelm Böhmens.

III. Der Berg-Predigt Christi/ und Gebettern vor die noch dahin auf dem Weg begriffenen rc.

IV. Königl. Englischen deswegen nach Teutschland erlassenen Abmahnung.

V. Kurtzen Relation, jenen dabey erlittenen Elendes und Schicksals.

VI. Noch einer andern Relation davon.

VII. Einem Stück der Warnungs-Predigt von Hn. Johann Tribecko rc. den zurückreisenden in London gehalten.

Alles aus Liebe zur Warheit und patriotischem Wohlmeinen zusammen verfasset.

Franckfurt und Leipzig / M DCC XI.

greater confusion, that in the presence of those encamping, especially those on the Blackheath, many thousands of white birds like doves, gathered, and after they had flown about in the sky for a few days, they died there and were buried by those that were left, in the cool sand. Thereupon the Englishmen ventured all sorts of conjectures and waited ever after for a fulfillment of their conjectures.

Finally in the year never to return, 1709, on the 6th and 8th of May, eleven ships filled with Germans arrived in the great and mighty city of London, in the neighborhood of St. Catharine's and the Royal Brewery, and there landed from them 18,006 persons, old men, young men and women, who after being sent to Blackheath, where the camp was laid out as before stated by the direction of the Queen, were ordered to lodge four by four in the tents provided for them.

A fortnight before the already named eleven ships arrived, five others had come bringing 4324 persons, transported from Holland to England, who also betook themselves to the camping place where they were kindly received by a nobleman through the gracious commands of the Queen. On St. John's Day four more ships arrived under full sail bringing 2138 souls, among whom were two clerical gentlemen, one named Master George Hainer, formerly vicar at Holtzen and Rudling, in the dominion of Lansenberg, and of the Evangelical Lutheran religion; the other was John Stager, a Reformed student from Nassau Siegen. He believed these 2138 were more highly regarded than any of the rest of the Germans, because they brought no Catholics with them, but at the command of their religious leaders debarred them from the ships. On this account they also received the best tents and the most pleasant location in the camp, namely the Rittercamp, and a more gracious eye was cast upon them than upon the others, by the wise Queen and the Parliament.

Six weeks after this three ships arrived in Greenwich haven with 1328 Germans, who had to go into the Middle camp by the wholesale, because they looked somewhat slovenly and had a good many Catholics among them.

About eight days before Michaelmas, (Sep. 29) the number of Germans was again increased by 4003 souls, part of whom took up their march at once into Ireland, partly because it was becoming colder. (We have not taken into account the 3060 men, women and children who were buried at Blackheath.) They were in the meantime lodged in St. Catharine's and in the Royal Brewery. At last, three days before St. Martin's Day, (Nov. 11) the camp was removed. The beginning was made with the Rittercamp, because the Lord Commissioners had sought out the best lodgments for them. More than one hundred wagons were sent to take our beggarly property from the camp, so that none had to work or incur expense. For eight days we had to take up our quarters in the Redhouse, until the rooms at Charles Cox's warehouse were cleaned. During the following eight days, while we were standing outside the Rittercamp at the Redhouse, two other ships arrived with 945 souls, who were at once directed to take up winter quarters in the above named warehouse.

Two ships were driven out of their course by a storm and these did not arrive until the second Sunday in Advent, and then only with 540 persons. The above named were sent to Westforth in order to have good quarters and not to further suffer as they had already done on the sea. In the Christmas week there was a report that some of the very richest men in Germany came to England, but in truth they were only corrupted Swiss and a few from Nassau Siegen. They had a few old horses, which I believe they would have eaten because of their great hunger.

There were 288 souls scattered about the streets by the Tower, where 168 large pieces of cannon were placed, which, as was customary, were fired when ships coming across the sea, arrived in the harbor.

At New Year 72 souls came over land about 100 miles, they having been deceived and brought hither on Holland coal ships.

After these there arrived by packet boat at one time 20, at

another 30, now more, now less, until the total number of Germans was 32,468 souls.

In order that I may take up again my former thought, I desire to inform the reader how it fared with the rest of these in camp in the taking up of winter quarters. First, the Catholics in the remaining camps were separated from the Lutherans and Reformed, and for a few days they were encamped by themselves. Then the gracious will of the Queen was made known to them. If they would enter the Protestant fold, they would secure the royal favor and protection, but if they decided to cling to their idolatrous religion, they might as well make up their minds to return to the Fatherland at once. They should have their free-will in the matter, because, inasmuch as the English people were alarmed at the growth of the Papacy, they were obliged to be on their guard lest it should get too much power; they could hardly do otherwise. Whereupon 3584 Catholics resolved to return to their homes again. After this resolution was made known, each of these persons received ten Reichs guelden as expense money on their way, and were placed on eight ships that they might be carried to Holland. The 520 Catholics who remained in England, became Protestant; 322 becoming Lutherans and the rest Reformed.

After this separation, the Middle camp also broke up and moved into the Redhouse, where the first ones had just quitted their quarters and sailed on the Thames to Battle Bridge to the warehouse of Mr. Charles Cox, with all their property. It was indeed a most excellent opportunity to pick out the Germans among them. The above named camp on Blackheath followed the Middle one into the Redhouse and then there were in all 17,000 souls to spend the winter together. In order that they might get along well, an overseer selected from their number belonging to a noble German family was given complete authority over them. He was made a general sanitary inspector and supervisor of the cooking booth.

Continuous envy and contention arose among the women while cooking. One would say to another in a threatening tone,

Kirchen-Ordnung,

Der Christlichen und der ungeänderten Augspurgischen Confession Zugethanen

Gemeinde in LONDON,

Welche,
Durch Göttliche Verleyhung,
Im 1694. Jahre,
Am 19. Sonntage nach dem Fest der Heiligen Dreyfaltigkeit,
Solenniter eingeweyhet und eingesegnet worden,

In St. Mary's Savoy.

Ep. 1. Cor. 14. v. 33. 40.
GOtt ist nicht ein GOtt der Unordnung, sondern des Friedens, wie in allen Gemeinen der Heiligen. Lasset es alles ehrlich und ordentlich zugehen.
Rom. 15. v. 33.
Der GOtt des Friedens sey mit euch allen! Amen.

Gedruckt im Jahr 1708.

"you wicked beggar, get out of this place, this is my hole and you shall not cook here." Then they would seize hold of each other by the hair and strike each other so that frequently the soup, meat and vegetables were spilt upon the ground, and it was evident that an overseer was needed. He took charge of the apartments of the women and put an end to their contentions.

The Straw commissioner gave these poor people fresh straw every two weeks on which to lie down. He was also a coal distributor, since, as it was somewhat rainy about Christmas, the Queen allowed a distribution of coal by the ship load to the poor people, that they might warm themselves.

The last of the camps to break up was the Camberwell which moved to Retriff. A few of them, as in the case of the Redhouse, stopped in Seventh street, and several hundred in St. Stephen. Those who had some provisions, remained here and there in London after their own pleasure, since they could stop comfortably with their own people.

Reaching the place of their entertainment, they were all so treated and accommodated, that no one could with reason complain of anything. Two hundred thousand pounds sterling or five millions, (?) the most gracious Queen Annie gave to us poor people.

Upon reaching the ship which was going to Rotterdam, we were taken in the best manner from England, at the expense of the Queen, with bread, beer, butter, bacon and cheese, and as God himself soon brought us over the sea, the Lord Commissioners were dispatched in the name of the Queen and the whole Parliament to congratulate us. After wishes of good luck had been given, each man received a nine pound loaf of bread, white as snow, and also a Reich gulden in money. We were then ordered to camp in the field and received weekly so much that every man could live respectably. All this they received from the Queen, besides what the princes, counts, barons, merchants and rich citizens daily spent for us. On many days, thirty and even more wagons loaded with bread and cheese were brought into camp, where, there being no purchasers, these

THE STATE OF THE PALATINES FOR Fifty YEARS past TO THIS PRESENT TIME.

CONTAINING,

I. An Account of the Principality of the *Palatinate*; and of the Barbarities and Ravages committed by Order of the *French* King upon the Inhabitants; Burning to the Ground a great Number of their most Famous Cities, and throwing the Bones of Emperors, Princes and Prelates, out of their Tombs, &c.

II. The Case of the *Palatines*. Publish'd by themselves, and Humbly Offered to the Tradesmen of *England*. With a List of them, and the Trades which the Men are brought up to.

III. The Humble Petition of the Justices of *Middlesex* to Her Majesty on their Behalf, with Her Majesties Order thereupon, and an Abstract of the Brief graciously Granted for their Subsistence.

IV. A Letter about Settling and Employing them in other Countries.

V. A Proclamation of the *States-General* for Naturalizing all Strangers, and receiving them into their Country.

VI. Lastly, Their present Encamping at *Camberwell* and *Black-heath*, in many Hundred Tents, by Her Majesties Grace and Favour, till they can be otherwise dispos'd of, and how they Employ themselves; with their Marriages, Burials, &c. Also the great Kindness their Ancestors shew'd to the *English* Protestants in the Bloody Reign of Queen *Mary*.

(See note 1.)

---

[1] This is another of those rare little booklets called forth during the sojourn of the Palatines in Great Britain. Its aim is fully expressed in the title. It is quite rare, but a few copies being in the libraries of this country. Through the courtesy of the State Library of New York, at Albany, I have been enabled to make myself master of its contents. I hereby desire to make public acknowledgment to the Officers of the said Library for having with the utmost readiness placed the book at my disposal. Only persons engaged in work like this can appreciate such favors properly.

things were freely distributed. Besides this, many rich gentlemen brought 60 or 80 pounds or as many Reichthalers and distributed them among the entire German people, and while doing so, said very modestly, "Take this now, with my Sympathy."

Many thousands of naked, and also such as out of greed locked up their own clothing in their chests, and went about in rags, were clothed anew.

A single business man, a Quaker, had for eight days cut up many wagon loads of cloth, for the naked ones. Another one bought out nearly all the Shoemakers; even before, he had bought 32.000 pairs of shoes which he gave to the people. And still another distributed 18,489 shirts so that those who were ill-clad might go better dressed. It would be hard to say how much the court preacher, now an inspector at Magdeburg, John Tribekko, spent in behalf of the Germans.

On the whole, our weak tongues can never tell the excellent deeds of charity which we Germans in England enjoyed. But sighing, we can only pray to God, that he may return it to them a thousand fold.

And likewise, as pure wheat is never entirely without weeds, or seldom a herd which has not one sickly member, so also among these many rich benefactors there were at times wicked outcasts who made it all the more bitter for the Germans. But the trouble came mostly by means of those Catholics who we previously had with us. At one time, while we were still camping in the fields, there came more than 1800 English people, on a dark night, with scythes and other weapons to our camp, who desired to cut down all the Catholics. This, indeed, without doubt would have been accomplished had they not been with the Lutherans and Reformed. To this day, on December 4 (1711) the pope is burned in effigy in all the streets of the city of London, and in all England, showing thereby how favorable they must have been to the Catholics!

Among the other dissolute outcasts there was a Presbyterian, born of the devil, a clerical, one devoid of all common sense, who had run away from Switzerland, and was now seeking to make it very bitter for these Germans. He represented them to the Queen and Parliament as wearing blue stockings, and declaring they should be allowed to perish like dogs. As he received but little attention, he placed himself behind the recruiting officers, and as if he had royal authority, took away the finest and youngest boys as soldiers on the men of war and in other military service, and swore like a common foot soldier. He indulged in tobacco, beer and whisky from morning until night, and had, like Sminderides for 20 years, or so long as he had been in England, never seen the sun rise or set, sober. In such a prolonged carousal he pleased all the poor Englishmen. He took away the children from the poor Germans, and played with them as a Jew would do. For when a poor Englishman obtained a child to whom he promised to teach his profession, the Queen gave him five pounds sterling : when they had the money they supported the child very well for a week or two, but after that gave him blows instead of bread, so that because of his extreme hunger he was forced to run away.

Finally, after such religious malice was discovered, it was made known to the public and upon the knowledge of this Pharaoh-like oppression, there began the German emigration from England to other countries and islands, bringing them to dire distress. The beginning of this movement was made by those who went into Ireland, numbering 3688 persons. They were badly accommodated. They had to endure hunger and cold keep several fast days every week, as they had nothing to eat. No one ever received anything he could call his own. He might go wheresoever he would, but he must remain, together with his own people, a slave and a bondsman.

First those in Liverpool followed those who had gone over into Ireland at the breaking up of the camp. Or rather 30 families or 126 persons of those in Liverpool followed after them. They were very excellent people, and artisans but were so well supported by their hard labor, that after they had consumed their own provisions they could drive away hunger. Sixteen families went into Sunderland, 120 miles from London, to a

Appendix F.   397

Prince who promised them so much ground, but did not keep his promise. Instead, he made day laborers of them and at last even went so far as to make those who did not escape in the night, slaves, sending them to Jamaica. Ten families proceeded to the West Country, otherwise called Plymouth, to earn their bread, in the Alaunen mountains. They received plenty of work but little pay. Now an Englishmen in those days received a Reich gulden for his daily wages, but the Germans only got a half Kopfferstücke. Thereupon they all turned their faces towards London, so that they might go back to Germany again.

Two families or fourteen people went to a gentleman 40 miles from London, at a place called Northumberland, who received only one pound of salt weekly among them, and daily they received half a pound of bread. Besides this they received neither meat nor vegetables of any kind. One family numbering eight was taken to a certain gentleman in the country, who promised them golden mountains, but in reality compelled them to herd swine. The head of this family was a hunter and an excellent man of the Reformed religion, and whose name I could give for the information of his friends. But he has escaped with wife and children, and with the others, who perhaps were not allowed to return to the Fatherland, went to New York.

Eight hundred and forty-four poor persons from Switzerland were put on board a ship to sail to North Carolina, but were anchored half a year at Portsmouth in the greatest hunger. 3086 persons were embarked on ten ships to be transported to New York, but they were already on the sea for eighteen weeks, from Christmas to Easter, and will leave port only with the fleet. It was their intention to enter some humble employment and if they could earn enough to buy property, they would become landholders. 1600 persons were packed on two ships to go to the Scilly islands, but when the inhabitants of that place received news of their coming, they sent a woefully worded petition to Parliament stating they could not support themselves much less the Germans, who did not understand fishing and

A BRIEF HISTORY OF THE Poor *Palatine* Refugees, Lately Arriv'd in ENGLAND.

Containing,

I. A full Answer to all Objections made against receiving them; and plain and convincing Proofs, that the Accession of Foreigners is a manifest Advantage to *Great Britain*, and no Detriment to any of her Majesty's native Subjects.
II. A Relation of their deplorable Condition; and how they came to be reduc'd to such Extremities.
III. A Description of the Country from whence they came.
IV. An Account of their Numbers.
V. By what Methods they have been subsisted.
VI. How they may be dispos'd of, to the Honour and Service of the Queen's Majesty, the Glory and Profit of this Kingdom, and the Advantage of themselves and Posterities. And
VII. An exact List of the Names of the Commissioners and Trustees appointed by her Majesty, for receiving and disposing of the Money to be collected for the Subsistance and Settlement of the said *Palatines*.

In a LETTER to a Friend in the Country.

LONDON Printed: And Sold by *J. Baker* at the *Black Boy* in *Pater-Noster-Row*, 1709. Price 6d.

(See note 2 on page 399.)

could not ward off hunger. After six weeks had passed they were again set on land, and went to Germany again accompanied by their Lutheran pastor.

Three hundred and twenty two young people went into the English military service. The English bought 141 children, boys and girls. Fifty six young persons were used as servants, besides these there were other families here and there that no one knew of, because they went out of the company without leaving their names. Of these there came back into Germany again, the following :

I. 3548 on the 29th of September, 1708 (1709?) went back to the Fatherland again.

II. 1600 who were to go to the Scilly islands went back again.

III. The 746 who were ordered to go to Ireland, had to go to Germany.

IV. 800 from Ireland came also upon German soil again.

In a like manner all those who escaped from Plymouth, Sunderland, Liverpool, and other places were also sent out of England. In all, these numbered 6994 souls. To Ireland, North Carolina, New York and other places, 8213 were sent. This number must be added to those who had gone into Germany, making a total of 15,201. The whole number that came to England was 32,468, and subtracting from this total the before

---

[1] This little book of 50 pages is one of the most valuable contributions to the history of my subject, I have found. It came into my hands more than six months after this article had been prepared, and while it contains little that I had not found in detached fragments elsewhere, it is nevertheless one of the fullest, and as I believe one of the most reliable of all the authorities that have survived the mutations of two centuries. The copy I have used is the property of Judge Pennypacker, who received it from his London agent only a few months ago. In my searches through some of the principal libraries of the country, I did not find a copy, and had no knowledge of its existence until its contents were placed at my service by its generous owner. It is possibly unique, and it were well, perhaps, if the Pennsylvania-German Society, should some day publish the little book entire.

mentioned 15,201 there were in all 17,261 who died in London and other parts of England, not taking into account the 200 who went down with the ship and those who were buried at sea and in Holland.

As long as the Germans were encamped, things went tolerably well in spite of the fact that most of the parents permitted their innocent children to become corrupt, and cared not if they died, not even going to their funerals. But there were other good people who buried them. To these funerals many hundred Englishmen went, both on foot and in wagons. Frequently the concourse made such a noise, both by the neighing of the horses, rattling of wheels and by their loud talking, that no one could hear the minister or schoolmaster who officiated.

As those still living were moved into quarters, a hundred or more together, and lodged there, one could then see among other things what these wicked people brought from Germany, who left their own people without counsel, help or comfort, to die like cattle. They did not bury their children decently but permitted them to be dragged along like carcasses. Ordinarily, at 2 o'clock in the afternoon, a signal was given to bury the dead, by means of sheep and cow bells, whereupon the men, two by two brought the corpse of an adult, hanging from a sort of a carrying frame, and these were followed by the corpses of the small and half-grown children, borne upon the heads of women, to the cemetery at Dertforth.[10] Perhaps half a dozen old women accompanied these funeral processions. (Weiber die mit in Engeland Würtz nägelein in Carolin zulesan gekommen.) As soon as the procession reached the cemetery, the corpses were thrown into a hole in layers, like herring. First were laid the women and virgins; upon these men and young boys, and upon these were placed the children, lengthwise and crosswise, until the hole was full.

---

[10] This practice is pursued in some Spanish American countries at the present day, with the accompaniments of men firing salutes from muskets and others playing on violins.

Appendix F.

Frequently it happened that when they carried out the dead and there were no ditches ready, they were put into coffins made of old boards and placed behind the encampment walls, from which they were taken by the dogs and entirely devoured. [—gantzlich aus den Sargen heraus nahmen und von ihnen Speisten.]

Those who were in other quarters, as the Redhouse, and remained with the Lutheran ministers, had it far better, for they were buried in a Christian manner, with beautiful hymns and a funeral panegyric. These services were usually conducted by Master George Hainer and the Schoolmaster, John George Tiltz. Rightly it was said of the Palatines, for so the Germans were commonly called in England, "you hit them, but they do not feel it." For if the evil Spirit choked and killed them, there was nothing but rejoicings and marriages among them. The before mentioned George Hainer himself joined 248 couples, and it is not definitely known how many were married by the others, namely by Master John Tribekko and Mr. Ruperti, before his arrival. 308 children were baptized by Mr. Hainer, five of whom were illegitimate, and thirteen were baptized at sea.

Nor should the remarkable marriage act be passed over in silence, which Mr. Hager accomplished after his ordination. Truly, he who could have seen this marriage ceremony performed as I saw it, would have laughed until his belly shook. In the first place, as Mr. Hager took his position in front of an old barrel full of cobbler's wax, and had mumbled a few words, a bridegroom came up who was lame in his left foot, accompanied by his bride, who was lame in the right foot. Truly they looked like children of Vulcan. Along with these came another couple, a very loving pair. The bride was more than 60 years old and had a hundred thousand wrinkles, in which foxes and hares could have hidden themselves; in other respects she looked much like a stuck calf. The groom was 18 or 19 years old, not yet dry behind the ears. He supported himself at the girdle of the bride, much like a child when it is learning to

Canary-Birds Naturaliz'd

IN

UTOPIA.

A CANTO.

Dulce est paternum solum.

LONDON

Printed : And sold by the Booksellers.
Price Six-pence.

(See note 3.)

Appendix F. 403

walk. The third pair, however, looked a little more graceful. The groom on account of sickness, was so weak he could hardly stand. The bride had a large eye and a small one, and was barefooted and ragged. Meanwhile, she would cast furtive glances upon her beautiful "Corydon" like a cat upon a mouse. This most honorable couple wound up the company as they were all gathered around the barrel. The minister spoke a few words and then they were all joined. Whereupon they all went

---

[3] While a number of brochures and booklets were written for and in the interests of the Palatines in England, a few were also written from an opposing standpoint, and this is one of them. It is more curious than meritorious. It is however exceedingly rare, the one whose title page is photographed above being the only copy I have ever seen. It belongs to Judge Samuel W. Pennypacker, in whose library great rarities and early Americana are as numerous as second-hand novels at a street bookstall.

The booklet is a protest against the encouragement, naturalization and establishment of the Palatines in Great Britain, and the argument is presented in the form of a story. The foreign interlopers are called canary birds, and a council of native birds is called to take action in the matter. The robin, the sparrow, the linnet, the lark, nightingale and the rest meet in council and in their most melodious strains show up the bad character of the canaries, and declare themselves opposed to affording them entertainment. But many other birds dissented. The crow, magpie, goose and eagle upheld the cause of the foreign canaries, and the latter triumphed. Of course the existing factions, interests and prominent persons are represented under these allegorical names, but who is intended can only be surmised.

With a few brief extracts, I shall dismiss this rare example of the Palatine literature of the period.

> In our unhappy Days of *Yore*,
> When foreign Birds from *German* Shore
> Came flocking to *Utopia's* Coast
> And o'er the Country, rul'd the Roast.
> We bought 'em dear, and fed 'em well
> 'Till they began for to rebel.
>
> *   *   *   *   *   *
>
> Or shall such Interlopers come
> And turn me out of House and Home?

away from each other, like goats when they go away from their shepherd, each one to his own place.

Now, at last, when everybody was married that could go or stand, their hopes were disappointed because Parliament would not give its consent to what the Queen had promised. Upon this, the preachers were ordered by the committee to make known in sermons and at prayer-meeting, that those who desired to return to the Fatherland, should so decide and give their

> Besides they're not of our Religion
> No more than any *Holland* Widgeon.
>
> * * * * * *
>
> Perhaps in Time they'll take, forsooth
> The Bread out of our Natives Mouth,
> To nat'ralize 'em is a Jest
> Lets not defile our own dear Nest.
>
> * * * * * *
>
> And will these Foreigners be found
> To till your waste and barren ground?
> In good Mechanics their Trades follow
> And let your fruitful Fields lie fallow.
> We've Poor enough among ourselves;
> Need no encroaching foreign Elves.
>
> * * * * * *

Here is a tilt at William Penn:

> At this, a quaking *Bird* o' the Feather
> Native, was highly nettl'd whether
> We'd nat'ral such vast Flocks together;
> Or how we'd of them so dispose
> As not to make intestine Woes;
> But on the Wing his ruffl'd Pen
> Was quickly set to Rights again,
> And by advancing his Dominion
> Made the best Feather in his 'Pinion.
> For presently the higher Pow'rs
> Prevail'd by plying the next Oars;
> To stop his mouth they found a way
> And sent them to 'Sylvania.

Appendix F. 405

names, for each one was to receive a **pound sterling for the expenses of the journey.** Upon this more than 900 people gathered together and returned again to Germany. The rest who remained in England, thought they would stay there, as it was a country in which the earth was so fruitful, that in many respects it could be compared to the promised land. In a word, it was an earthly Paradise. Yet good and excellent as the land was, in spite of it all, the Germans were forced to make room and go again upon German soil. But the most of these people went to Dantzig. How contented they all will be there, experience will tell us.

APPENDIX G.

ANOTHER ACCOUNT OF THE STAY OF THE PALATINES IN AND AROUND LONDON —DETAILS OF THE MEASURES ADOPTED TO SUBSIST THEM DURING THEIR STAY AND TO PROVIDE FOR THEIR PERMANENT SETTLEMENT.[13]

SEAL OF WILLIAM PENN.

HER Majesty being informed of the miserable Condition of these People, was at the whole Charge of transporting them into her own Dominions, and took particular Care of their Subsistence; but their Numbers being like to increase, and it must necessarily take up some Time for appointing and settling the Distribution of her Majesty's Charity for their daily Relief, a certain Number of well disposed private Gentlemen, Divines, Physicians, Merchants and Characters, whose names I have no authority to publish, and

---

[13] Palatine Refugees in England, p. 30.

Appendix G.

whose indefatigable Pains and unexemplify'd Charities, nothing less than Heaven can recompense, voluntarily, and without any Invitation or Motive, but their own pious Inclinations obliging them to it; 1st, Because the Palatines were in great Distress. 2dly, Because they were Strangers; And 3dly, Because it was not known that the Government, or any else provided, for them. In which good Offices they laboured abundantly and effectually, from about the Middle of May, till the 2d of July, at which time Commissioners were appointed by her Majesty's Letters Patent, to take Care of 'em, and receive Proposals for the Disposal of 'em, whereof all these private Gentlemen aforesaid, are of the Number.

In order to make Provision for these distressed People, when these Gentlemen acted in a private Capacity, they first met in a room in the Temple Change Coffee House, and afterwards at a Gentleman's Chambers in the Queen's-Bench Walks, in the Temple, where they erected themselves into a Charitable Society, elected a Chairman, and came to such Resolutions as were thought most expedient for the Subsistence of the Palatines. To which End they chose two Agents to attend these People *de Die in Diem*, to inform themselves and then the Gentlemen, of their Several Conditions, and to distribute the private Charities in such Proportion as they saw convenient, 'till Places might be found to lodge them in, without any trouble to the Inhabitants; and besides these Particulars, by their Interest with the Nobility, Gentry, Merchants and others, they procur'd as much private Charity from several Hands, during the short Time of their acting as private Gentlemen, as amounted to between 7 and 800 Pounds; Many of which Benefactors, in Obedience to that Evangelical Precept, of not letting the left Hand know what the right Hand does, in this kind, conceal'd their Names from this Charitable Society; tho' the Gentlemen never omitted returning their hearty thanks to the Benefactors by the Persons that brought it.

The private Charities thus Collected, these Gentlemen ordered to be put into the Hands of a Goldsmith, which was employ'd for the Subsistence of the Distressed; and whereas several of them, at their first coming were in great Want, all imaginable Care and Speed was us'd to procure them Lodging by their Agents, the number of whom they encreas'd with the Number of the Palatines, to whom they allow'd and pay'd 12s. per week for their Pains and Subsistence, besides other necessary Charges and Expenses in the Service of the necessitous Palatines.

About this Time, viz. May 23, 1709, there was an estimate produc'd, that the Number of the Palatines were 825 Men, Women and Children, residing about the Tower, St. Cathrenes, Tower Ditch, Wapping, Nightingale Lane, East Smithfield and Places adjacent, whereupon it was agreed by the Gentlemen to thin the Number, by hiring some cheap Houses and Barns out of the Town; which was done accord-  ingly, and they were lodg'd in Barns and Houses at Kensington, Walworth, Stockwell, Bristol, Cansey, and Camberwell; and as the Number of the Palatines encreas'd, so did the Care of these Gentlemen, in providing more Barns and Houses for them; also in procuring from the Queen Lodging for them in her Majesty's Rope Yard at Deptford, in the upper Rooms in the Red House in the same Place, which the Queen hir'd and were then vacant, with the Loan of a thousand Tents from her Majesty, for their Reception on Blackheath, Greenwich and Camberwell, where a Gentleman of that place gave a Ground to set them up in. Nor did the Care of these Gentlemen terminate in Lodging them, but they also suppli'd them with great Quantities of Bread, Cheese, Milk and Small Beer with Straw to lie on, Blankets and Cover-lids and as many Combs as cost £12.

They also took Care when any of the Palatines were sick, to provide Necessaries fit for them in such a Condition, and a

THE PENNSYLVANIA-GERMAN SOCIETY.

learn'd and charitable Physician of their own Number, took the Pains to visit them, and supply'd them with Physical Medicaments at his own Expense, as well as leaving a Chirurgeon behind him, to administer them according to his Direction.

But all these being corporal Charities, these Gentlemen ceas'd not here, but also made Provision for Spiritual Food for their Souls : and to that pious End, agreed with Mr. Sc——r to read Prayers to the Palatines every Day, for which he was to be allow'd the Charge of his Coach-hire; the Clerk of the Prussian chappel was to assist at divine Service, and to be consider'd for his Pains. To farther improve their knowledge in the Word of God, these Gentlemen desir'd one of their Number to write to his correspondent at Hamburg, to buy and send over a thousand High Dutch New Testaments, and the Psalms in Prose, in Quires in the Long Primer, for the Use of the Palatines, and order'd that £60 should be reserv'd to pay for them. Lastly, they agreed that it should be taken into Consideration, how to form a Proposal to the Government, for applying the Queen's Allowance to support five hundred Palatine Children, from the Age of six to twelve, at a Charity School, in order to be instructed to write and read English, to be taught their Catechism, to cast Accompt, and to work on the Linnen Manufactures, &c. And now these private Gentlemen having voluntarily done all these great and charitable Offices for the Palatines, they put an End to their Meeting in the Temple, and the Trustees appointed by her Majesty to distribute the Money collected for the Palatines, met the first Time, viz. July 2d at the New Building joining the Banquetting House, and adjourn'd themselves to the next Wednesday Morning at St. Paul's Chaple House. * * * * *

ARMS OF CHUR—BRAUNSCHWEIG.
1694.

The Queen's great Charity has, ever since the first Arrival of the Palatines, been the principal Fund for their Subsistence, the other Charities, though they did abundance of Good, as an additional Relief, by the prudent Management of the Gentlemen, yet they were but precarious, and not to be rely'd upon; so that her Majesty's Charge, by the Increase of these Foreigners, was raised from £16 a Day, at first, to £100 a Day afterwards ; which was distributed by the two German Divines (that only had Authority to dispose of it) in this Proportion, viz. To each Man, and each Woman above twenty Years of Age five Pence. To those under twenty, and above ten, four Pence. To those under ten Years of Age, three Pence *per diem*, which was pay'd every Tuesday and Friday, besides one Pound of Bread *per diem* to each of 'em : but there being only two Gentlemen, as has already been said, that had Authority to receive and dispose of the Queen's Charity, to whom it grew a greater Burden then they were able to bear, it was thought convenient by the Ministry, to put the care of the Palatines under a due Regulation, by authorizing a Number of Persons, fitly qualify'd, to enquire into their State, and the properest Measure for their Relief and Settlement ; whereupon her Majesty was graciously pleased to appoint Commissioners and Trustees ; by her Letters Patents under the Great Seal, for Collecting, receiving, and disposing of the Money to be collected for the Subsistence and Settlement of the poor Palatines, who upon July 6, 1709, gave publick Notice in the *Gazette*, that they would meet in a general Meeting in the Chapter House of St. Pauls, on every Wednesday at four of the Clock in the afternoon, and that in order to receive Proposals for employing and settling the said Palatines, and to prepare Business for the said general Meeting, they would meet as a Committee in the new Buildings adjoining to the Banquetting House in Whitehall, on every Tuesday, Thursday, and Saturday, at four of the Clock in the afternoon ; and that they would also meet as a Committee in the Council Chamber in Guild-hall, London, on every Monday and Friday at four of the clock in the Afternoon, and on every Wednesday at ten of the Clock in the Morning, the first of the said Meetings to be on the Friday following.

APPENDIX H.

ARMS OF CITY OF AUGSBURG.

IN the rare book belonging to Judge Pennypacker of which I have already spoken,[10] I found the following summary of the persons who left Germany during this Exodus, as well as the places from which they emigrated. How the writer who prepared it was able to get at the exact numbers it is difficult to say at this distant day, and yet, it is possible his figures may be approximately correct. It will be observed the sum total does not reach the half of that of the writer quoted in Appendix F.

F. R. D.

LISTE DER NACH DER INSEL PENSYLVANIEN ABGEREISTEN LEUTE.

Aus der Pfaltz	8,589
Aus dem Darmstattichen	2,334

[10] Das verlangte, nicht erlangte Canaan.

Aus dem Hanauischen	1,113
Aus dem Francken-Land[1]	653
Aus dem Mahntzischen[2]	63
Aus dem Trierischen[3]	58
Aus dem Speyrischen, Wormsischen und Graffschafftlichen[4]	490
Aus dem Hessenland[5]	81
Aus dem Zweybrückischen[6]	125
Aus dem Nassauischen[7]	203
Aus dem Elsass	413
Aus dem Baadischen[8]	320
Aus allerhand Landschaften ledige Hand-wercks Leute	871
Summa	15,313

ANOTHER SUMMARY, TO JUNE 10, 1709.[11]

By June 10, there had come over the following:

Men that had families	940
Unmarried men	292
Daughters above fourteen years of age	247
Sons under fourteen years	1016
Wives	903
Widows	73
Unmarried women	77
Sons above fourteen years	257
Daughters under fourteen years	950
A Total of	4,774

---

[1] Land of the Franks. Now belonging to Bavaria, called Kreise or counties; Ober, Mittel and Unter Franken, including the cities of Nuremberg, Baireuth and Würzburg.

[2] The Archbishopric of Mayence (Mainz).

[3] The Archbishopric of Trier.

[4] The Ecclesiastical districts of Speir, Worms and Grafschaftlich of the Palatinate Rhine Provinces.
[5] From Hesse Darmstadt (Electorate.)
[6] From the district of Zweibrücken, a city of the Palatinate.
[7] From Hesse-Nassau (Cassel) Electorate.
[8] From Baden.
[11] State of the Palatines, p. 7.

Evening Reception.

During the evening a most notable and enjoyable reception was given by the Historical Society of Pennsylvania to the visiting members of the Pennsylvania-German Society at the rooms of the former, 1300 Locust street, Philadelphia, Pa., which was largely attended by many members of both Societies, prominent in their several communities and distinguished throughout the country at large.

By unanimous vote the thanks of the Society were heartily tendered the Historical Society of Pennsylvania for this and the many other courtesies shown during their Annual meeting in Philadelphia.

www.ingramcontent.com/pod-product-compliance
Lightning Source LLC
Chambersburg PA
CBHW020848160426
43192CB00007B/829